Perfectly Imperfect

Ellen Keane is a four-time Paralympian, who won a gold medal in the 100-metre breaststroke at the 2020 Paralympics in Tokyo. In 2022 she reached the final of *Dancing With the Stars* on RTÉ One. She is the recipient of a Lord Mayor of Dublin Award. This is her first book.

Liadán Hynes is a journalist and bestselling author of two books, *How to Fall Apart* and *Courting*. She is the host of the podcast *How to Fall Apart*, and lives in Dublin with her daughter.

Perfectly Imperfect

Embrace your DIFFERENCE,
Find your SUPERPOWER

Ellen Keane

with **Liadán Hynes**

Gill Books

Gill Books
Hume Avenue
Park West
Dublin 12
www.gillbooks.ie

Gill Books is an imprint of M.H. Gill and Co.

978 07171 9616 6

Designed by iota (iota-books.ie)
Print origination by Bartek Janczak
Edited by Esther Ní Dhonnacha
Proofread by Liza Costello
Printed and Bound in the UK using 100% Renewable Electricity at
CPI Group (UK) Ltd
This book is typeset in 12 on 18pt, Quixote.

The paper used in this book comes from the wood pulp of sustainably managed forests.

This book is not intended as a substitute for the medical advice of
a physician. The reader should consult a doctor or mental health
professional if they feel it necessary.

A CIP catalogue record for this book is available from the British
Library.

5 4 3 2 1

Contents

Introduction

As I am finishing this book, I'm about to begin training for my last Paralympic Games, Paris 2024. I'm so excited to get started, to enjoy this final year in a world I have felt is my home for many years.

I'm 28 now, and coming to the end of one massive chapter in my life: the swimming career I embarked upon when I was still a child, becoming the youngest ever Irish Paralympian at the age of 13 and winning a gold medal in Tokyo in 2021. But that said, there were many times in my life as I was growing up when I was struggling, and I had no one to talk to, and no one to turn to, and it felt like there was no one else who felt the way I was feeling.

Feeling alone made the difficult things I experienced so much worse; I believed no one had ever felt the same, this different, this other, not enough, and that made things so much harder. It was only when I began to speak out about how I was feeling that I learned I was not alone – far from it, in fact! In the greatest way possible, I wasn't special in the slightest – many people felt or had felt the same. That they were different, other, not enough. Ironically, my differences became a means of connection with others, a point of similarity, something I came to realise the more I shared about how I felt. Being open and vulnerable started to become something that brought comfort, rather than something scary.

If you are feeling alone, and different, and you can't find anyone in your world who seems to be experiencing the same thing, or you don't feel that you can, or want to, talk to anyone right now, I would like this book to be a comfort blanket for you. I hope that my story told here validates what you are feeling, and that this book is a place for you to turn to when you're feeling alone or conflicted. Hopefully you will be able to find something within these pages that might help set you on the right path.

I often get asked by people who also have a disability, or who might be feeling insecure about themselves in some way, what's the answer? How did I do it? How did I get the courage to start living a carefree life, and how did I learn to love my body?

At first, when people asked me these questions, I used to get a bit overwhelmed by the feeling that I had to have the answer. People were coming to me, and I needed to give them what was going to work. But, I came to realise, there is no one answer. Certainly nothing I could cover in a DM reply to an Instagram message!

Because the answer isn't straightforward. It was a slow process and there were a lot of factors involved. I went on a journey to accept my body, learning to accept myself, even discovering that I don't always have the answer, and that maybe I still have my own work to do on myself. It is an ongoing process.

Which brings us to this book. Rather than trying to answer each query individually, I wanted to put it all down here, a sort of guidebook to how I dealt with things, what I have learned works for me, and reflections on the times I struggled, so you can have it to refer to whenever you need, dip into whenever you find yourself also struggling.

Each chapter covers something that has been important to me along the way, a sort of building block, or something I needed to learn to deal with. At the end of each chapter are three challenges, small, medium and big, because this is how I like to break my goals up when I am setting them – building from the micro up to make larger changes. I would suggest picking a new notebook to use alongside the book as you read, to record observations, feelings or even changes in yourself you are noticing as you work through the chapter challenges. I hope by tackling these challenges, and using the notebook to record your progress, by the end of this book you will be further along on your own journey towards self-acceptance.

This book is a way of explaining how I got from feeling alone and isolated because of my difference to feeling like it is the best thing about me, my superpower. But it will also show the reality of my journey, because it's not like it happened overnight. There were so many highs – my gold medal, my time on *Dancing with the Stars* – but also, as you will see, so many lows. As I will explain in the chapters that follow, there is no quick fix.

I am not 100% all of the time, and I never will be. Who is? What I would like to do is humanise things, show you the truth of my story and how I came to self-acceptance, and to hopefully help you to realise that everything you need to do the same is already within you. I'm not special. That's the most important thing for me: to make people realise I'm not special. What I went through and what I did – everyone has those emotions, everyone has those feelings, and it's just about recognising them and learning how to deal with them. This book will show you how I recognised them, and how even the negative feelings, emotions and experiences I have had have all played their part in getting me to the place I am in now. Without them, I mightn't have had the amazingness that comes with everything else. I might have missed the best parts.

I was never bullied as a kid. A lot of the thoughts I had were my own internal ableism. And that was because I hadn't seen anyone who looked like me, so for many years I felt I was inherently wrong. Ever since I have learned to embrace my arm and my body, I've made it my mission to put myself out there as much as possible, and to try and be a role model, to be that person for other people with disabilities to look at and think, *if she can do it, I can do it.* Visibility is so important.

It's not just disabled people who I've connected with. It's anyone who has had any sort of insecurity, anyone who has felt like they haven't belonged. I want this book to be the person I needed when I was a kid, a teenager, or even older. For anyone who feels similarly, I want it to be that for you too, now, in the moment.

I know how bad the demons in your head can get, how paralysing thoughts can be, how you might not even recognise the extent of the negative self-talk you're subjecting yourself to. I want to highlight the power of the negative, but also of the positive things you can say to yourself. And to look at all the things that are in your control which you can do to make yourself feel better, the pillars of your life that will help you to love yourself.

I want this book to be nearly like a best friend that you can turn to when you don't have anyone else to talk to. I have a wonderful, loving family, but the thing about me and my arm is that I never told anyone that I was scared, or about the thoughts I was having. I'm not sure, even if I had wanted to, that I could have; I didn't even understand exactly what I thought. I just knew I had to hide, rather than embrace who I was. And I knew I felt as if I couldn't be loved, that I was unworthy. These were all things that I kept in. I couldn't tell anyone because I felt like no one would understand. So I want this book to be something that you can relate to, and hopefully, a place where you will feel understood.

A place where you can find yourself, which means you don't have to turn to someone if you don't want to. You can turn to this book and rely on it, as you might a good friend who you can talk to. Sometimes there's only so much talking to other people we can do, and at the end of the day it has to come from inside you. I want this book to help you with that.

I've gone to psychologists; I've gone to sports psychologists; I have access to so many people who could help me. But often I have found my strength and inspiration from the books that I read. I want this book to be that inspiration for anyone who reads it.

When you have a difference, adapting to situations is a skill that you learn from a very young age. So when things happen now, and there might be a bit of panic, I'm able to think outside the box a lot more easily than other people because I have learned there is always more than one way of doing something. People will often say to me, 'Oh, you've overcome your disability.' I hate that, because I haven't overcome my disability. The world isn't designed for disability, so I overcome ableism, every day.

Whenever I'm telling my story, my life seems to naturally divide up into chapters. Pre-Beijing, and the thirteen-year-old kid I was at those first Games in 2008. Then the years up to London in 2012, a teenager, struggling to balance wanting to do the things that everyone else was doing with needing to learn what was necessary to look after myself as an athlete.

Then between London and Rio, learning how to better physically mind myself. Becoming a better athlete, stronger, fitter. But then realising in Rio that I hadn't been minding myself mentally. And finally, the years between Rio 2016 and Tokyo 2020 (its official title, although it actually took place the following year) when I really started to understand how to do that.

The chapter I'm in now, I finally feel like I have all the tools. I'm going to retire from swimming this year, after my last Games in Paris, and I'm already looking forward to what comes next. Where before, a lot of my decisions were made for other people, or influenced by other people, at this point in my life it's as if I've come full circle, and I'm back to where I was when I was a kid; I am swimming because I love it. And as an adult, I feel like I am really learning how to love myself more. I do things for me, and I am comfortable in my own individuality. All those other Games, all those years, I was always so influenced by people around me, letting them make the decisions and just listening to them. Now, I have learned to listen to myself.

In sport they always say, 'Control the controllables.' In these pages, I have tried to capture the story of my controllables, the things I did, and still do, to get me where I am today: comfortable in myself. Embracing my difference, seeing my arm as my superpower. To track the ways I've managed various aspects of my life, in the hope that they might help you to feel how I feel today. Happy, strong, not afraid, not alone, finding the power in my difference, embracing who I am.

Perfectly Imperfect.

Love,
Ellen

one

Love

Perhaps,
we should learn to love
ourselves so loudly,
it silences our insecurities.

Louise Kaufmann

People often point out to me how relaxed I looked in the moments after I won the gold medal. It was in Tokyo, at the 2020 (2021) Paralympics. If you look back at the video, you can see how calm my face is. It's not that I wasn't happy, but in a way, I had known I was going to win. I had been building up to it for so long.

I think because I had spent so much time working towards it, even in the moment in Tokyo, after I'd won the gold medal, it was the weirdest feeling. You watch sport, and you watch people achieve their goals on TV all the time. There's this big dramatic exertion of emotion. And I didn't have that. What I had was a calmness. For ages, I was almost afraid to watch the video back, because I was afraid I'd never feel that calmness again.

Just before I dove into the pool that day, I told myself, 'No matter what happens, you'll be OK. I love you.' That was the first time that I ever *really* believed those words. And that is how I won a gold medal.

By the time I got to Tokyo in August, one year after the Games were initially planned, a date postponed because of Covid-19, I was in the habit of doing self-talk, especially every time I had a hard session. I would talk to myself encouragingly, and it would help me get through. Still, though, when it comes to the Games themselves, the pressure you feel in the lead-up, when you're actually in the village, then about to walk out, is very intense.

But on the day, I just kept saying to myself, 'There's no way I can't win gold here.'

In the call room before a race, I always listen to music. The room has chairs everywhere; it's where athletes wait before their races. Next is a smaller room where the two heats just about to race spend their final moments before getting in the pool. Sitting there, I was so relaxed. I was listening to Eminem – I had gotten into the habit of telling myself, 'I'm phenomenal,' every time I raced, listening to his song called 'Phenomenal'. I took the sentiment from it. That day, my playlist ran out before it was my turn to get in the water, and a Katy Perry song came on, unplanned. Called 'Unconditionally', it's about loving someone else unconditionally, but in that moment, I took it to mean that no matter what happened, I would love myself unconditionally. Sitting in that corridor, it gave me further peace of mind.

In that moment before getting into the water I felt completely relaxed. Even that song was another sign that I could trust that it was going to happen. So when it actually did, when I won gold, that's why I was so relaxed. Because I had just believed so much that it could happen.

Celebrating your difference

It all came together for me in those moments. But years of work, in the pool, and personally, in all aspects of my life, had gone into being able to meet this challenge with such conviction and self-belief. It's everything that made up that path over those years that I want to share with you here. All the things I did to get myself to that moment before diving into the water, when I was full of self-belief, self-love, trust in myself and my abilities. How I set goals, big and small. How I learned to love myself, to celebrate my difference.

When I dove into the water, my goggles filled up with water almost immediately, and I couldn't see a thing. Luckily in training I had counted my strokes, so I knew how many it would take me to get to the other wall, roughly 15 or 16. I mostly couldn't see the woman in the lane beside me, my main competition; I couldn't see anything at all. In hindsight, I think this was a good thing, because I couldn't panic. In the past I would have been really aware of other people around me. And where before, something like my goggles flooding might have thrown me, on that day, I knew I just had to focus on what I was doing. Nothing distracted me, and I was filled with self-belief.

LOVE

It was just another little happenstance that made me feel that everything was happening as it should. I wasn't meant to see what was going on. It meant I was laser focused.

When I finished my race, because my goggles were filled with water, all I could see was that my main competitor's block had two lights on it. I knew she was the closest one to me, that if anyone was going to beat me, it would have been her. Because her block had two lights, I knew my block would have one light.

I had come first. Gold.

My story

Growing up, as far as I could see there was nobody in the world who looked like me. Nobody I knew, no celebrity, nobody in the media, nobody with a body like mine who I could look up to.

When people thought of someone with a disability, they thought of someone who was in a wheelchair, or maybe blind or deaf.

I was born with one arm. I kind of forget now that people don't know my arm story; I don't know if I have even told my boyfriend the background. I don't talk about it that much anymore; I guess I spoke about it more in the beginning because I felt the need to. But I've been in the media a fair bit by now, so it had gotten to the point where I felt, *OK, people don't need to hear my story anymore.*

I'm the youngest of four, with an older sister, and older twin brothers. We grew up on Dublin's northside. I was born with my left arm missing from below the elbow. My parents, Eddie and Laura, hadn't known it was going to happen before I was born – it didn't show up in any scans. The story they told me is that my mam was very sick in the hospital just after I'd been born, so the first person to see me was my dad. There was a big fuss over me, and he didn't really understand what was going on; there was also a big fuss around my mam, just a lot of chaos.

When the nurse eventually brought me in for my dad to see me, my arm was pulsing and red. 'Oh, don't worry about that,' she told him. 'The doctor will be in in a second to sort that out.'

In the heat of the moment with everything that was going on, my dad thought a doctor was going to come in and some-how perform a magic trick where he just needed to maybe cut something, and an arm would appear. As he was probably quite overwhelmed by all that was happening, that was my dad's logic, because he hadn't been expecting any of this. And because it just wasn't a typical thing you would see. I suppose he hadn't yet had time to properly take it in.

Of course, the doctor didn't do anything to make an arm appear, and after a day or so, my dad brought me home. (My mam had to stay on in hospital for a short while longer before she was well enough to come home.) Obviously they were a bit shocked, but my parents have always been so good at just going, 'It is what it is.' They decided, 'OK, we're going to throw her in the deep end [excuse the pun] with her brothers and her sister. This is how it is, and she'll be fine.' And so I wasn't treated any differently.

And mostly, for my primary school years, I *was* fine. In fact, I was a really happy kid, who loved to play, who laughed a lot.

The medical term for being born with different limbs is *dysmelia*. My parents were never given a reason why it happened. But through my sport I've come across many girls with very similar arms to me – in the world of para sport it always seems to be girls who have one arm and boys who have one leg, I don't know why, and it always seems to be the left arm that's affected as well. In meeting these girls, I have heard various reasons for why this might happen.

One reason people are sometimes given is that the umbilical cord wraps around the arm in the womb and prevents growth. Another girl told me she poked her stump out of the amniotic sac, and that prevented the arm from growing. I know another girl who underwent a new method of prenatal genetic testing when her mom was pregnant; her mother was the first person to get this test done. The doctors were able to see something in her DNA that showed her arm wasn't going to grow.

Getting stuck in

Like I say, my parents were never given a reason why. I don't think any one of us has a specific right answer; there are just lots of possibilities as to what it could be.

Either way, I was treated exactly the same as my older siblings. I went to playschool, did lots of sports and activities. The only difference I knew compared to everyone else was that I went to Cappagh Hospital for rehab. I needed to learn how to use my hand a lot more: I remember that as a kid there was always Play-Doh for me to mess with, to strengthen my hand muscles.

I also got to be quite mobile with my left foot, to the point where I could use it as a hand. The doctor told my parents, 'Oh, as soon as she starts wearing shoes, she'll lose that dexterity, she won't be able to do it anymore,' but they were wrong; I'm still really flexible and dexterous with my left foot. I can pick things up with it, open doors. If I'm walking around the house and I need to pick up something, I will just lift it with my foot and then put it in my hand. I do this without even thinking about it – it's more of an automatic thing. I always thought everyone did that! But they don't. My right foot is completely useless compared to my left foot. It frustrates me so much!

My flexible left foot also helps me in the pool; it means I have more grip. For breaststroke, you turn your feet out and kick. I'm able to do that a lot more easily on the left than I am on the right. It means I need to do a lot more rehab exercises with my right foot to try and get the flexibility up to match my super-strong left foot.

Because of this, my foot means more to me. When I was doing *Dancing with the Stars*, I remember I hurt my foot at one point, and I was freaking out because for me, it's like my hand – I need it.

Going to rehab was the only big difference in my life compared to others as a child. I've always had a prosthetic, but my mam always gave me the option of whether or not to wear it – my parents never wanted to force it on me.

As a kid, I would always take it off and throw it around, which could sometimes lead to funny situations. One day when I was little, my mam took me with her to the supermarket. I was in the trolley, and I threw my prosthetic into the freezer with the peas and stuff. We moved on without my mam noticing, and then all of a sudden women were screaming at the freezer; they had spotted the prosthetic nestled amongst the bags of peas!

I didn't like having a prosthetic; I felt it wasn't me and instead was just getting in the way. My arm would get really sweaty, bacteria would build up, and I would get sores that were extremely painful. It's hard enough keeping a kid clean without having to think about prosthetics.

I remember my first day at school, going in I had a prosthetic on and we all brought our teddies in. I was happy and excited – that was generally the kind of kid I was in primary school. I don't remember feeling different. I would always leave for school with my prosthetic on and come back with it sticking out of my bag. (When I started going to the senior school, I had an electric arm so that I could cycle. It had sensors on either side and would open and close. But the battery would last for just half an hour, and after that it would be stuck on just closed or open, one or the other, and I wouldn't be able to use it anymore.)

I never felt othered or different in primary school. I wasn't insecure or aware of my arm like I later became in secondary school. I played GAA, did hip-hop and tap dancing. And obviously, I swam. Kids were never mean to me or anything. I was always surrounded by people who were so open to trying things another way.

With GAA, for example, I used to play for Scoil Uí Chonaill. To pass a ball, you have to hold the ball and then obviously hit it like that. I figured out my own method that worked for me, and that was absolutely fine.

The only time I ever felt excluded was when a substitute swim teacher made me wear an armband. That wasn't fun, and my mam went through her for it afterwards when she found out.

I guess I was vaguely aware that I was different, but I never felt othered, and, most importantly, being different didn't feel like it was a bad thing. I was just Ellen, a happy kid who loved to run around, who laughed a lot, who liked to play.

A lot of this is down to my parents. I think what they gave me, or the sense they created around me, was that there were never any barriers. It was only as I became an adult, moving out more into society and doing my own thing, that I started to see the barriers. Then, it was society and other people putting up these barriers. My parents had *never* put up any blocks; at no point when I asked if I could do something was no the answer. Their approach was always just about adaptation, and a matter of trying to figure out a way of doing something.

My dad comes from a really big family, he's one of seventeen, so he's always had to work hard. If he wanted something, he had to figure out a way of getting it. And I guess he was always competing with his siblings for whatever was going. So he is just so good at figuring out how to get things done. And then my mam was brilliant at nurturing, and making sure that I believed in myself.

My parents would get very defensive if someone said no to me. Because there was no reason why the answer should be no. When it's no, it's just a lack of imagination, and a lack of creativity. And fear as well. My parents have just never had that fear. It was always about possibility. I grew up really loved.

It was when I went to secondary school and moved into my teenage years that things started to change. I began to really feel my difference from everyone else – being different is the worst thing possible for a teenager – and I began to feel really insecure about my arm. I started to hide it, resting it behind my back in family holiday photographs, always wearing loose hoodies with long sleeves that would conceal my arm. My mental health began to suffer, and I became more and more silent: scared to talk up, afraid of confrontation, keen to fit in and pass through unnoticed, with no confidence whatsoever in my own views and opinions.

Finding my safe space

The pool became the only place where I felt safe. Amidst all the change of secondary school, the sense of being unlike everyone else, of never being enough, it was my constant. I found people there who are still to this day some of my best friends. People with whom I felt I belonged, a feeling that was missing in school.

When you train together like that, there's a sense of solidarity. You're in it together, the fun times and the hard times. No matter what the session or the set was, by the end of however long it lasted, we'd completed it together. So there's bonding, and joy that comes with it. There was also a sense of acceptance. My swim teammates never treated me any differently. They were just my family – that's how I feel about them and other people in the swimming world. I guess that's why I was a bit overwhelmed at my last World Championships in 2023, because professional swimming is my home, and it is also my family, and I'm going to miss it.

The pool was somewhere I never felt the need to hide myself; it would have been impossible even if I'd wanted to, stripped back as I was to swimsuit, goggles and hat. But I never felt the desire to hide who I was, or to conceal my body, in the pool. It was the place that showed me I could be confident, strong, make friends, achieve things, speak up, laugh, even when I felt I couldn't do these things anywhere else in my life. At times it was like living two different lives or being two different people, but even when I struggled, deep down there was always a part of me that knew I could be a happy, confident person, because I had experienced that as a kid, in the pool, at school, with my family.

In class in secondary school, I would hide my arm, covering it under a long sleeve. I constantly dreaded the reactions of others. Just the anticipation of that was as much a problem as the occasions themselves when someone would say something. The expectation of the next time keeping me in a state of anxious alert for when I would next be pulled sharply up and out of my day as I crashed into the ignorance, prejudice or just plain awkwardness of others' reactions to my body, and be made to feel different in front of my peers. The thing every teenager dreads was a constant possibility for me.

There is the time a teacher asks, 'What's wrong with your arm? Did you break it?'

The bell for the end of the class goes, and I run off, embarrassed. Someone else, a classmate, fills her in. And again, I am left feeling different, othered, and wondering if this is how everyone sees me. If all they see when they look at me is my disability – something I then felt very uncomfortable about.

Sometime after this, when I'm studying for my Leaving Cert in the Institute, a guy I have been friends with for a year asks one day in sixth year, 'Oh, did you break your arm?'

Me: 'No, I just don't have an arm.'

And his shocked expression, making me feel like a freak, and so small.

A boyfriend warning me out of the blue that I can no longer be friends with one of the other guys in our group. I am completely confused – what does he mean, I can't be friends with him anymore? It makes me cross. He isn't going to tell me who I can and can't talk to. He won't explain, but instead tells me just to leave it, that this guy is not a good person, and I should avoid him.

Later one of the girls in the group fills me in: they had all been sitting around one day when I wasn't there, and this boy had said, 'Oh yeah, Ellen would be hot if she had two hands.'

These kinds of things only served to confirm what I already assumed society was thinking about me. And were why I wanted to avoid people ever noticing me too much, why I preferred to go under the radar, because when someone did say something like that to me, straight away it would confirm what I thought people were thinking. It confirmed my fears. That I was different, and that there was something wrong with me, that I was less than. I remember once in sixth year, I was in a biology practical and my partner was on his way, but he was late. The teacher asked, 'Oh, where is your partner for this practical?'

I said, 'Oh, he's on his way in.'

And he replied, 'Oh, OK, good. Because you're already at a handicap.'

When people said things like that to me, it would jar me. *Handicap* is such an outdated term and it's an automatic negative. It's an automatic feeling of 'I'm less than'. It's that kind of thing that puts you in a constant state of hypervigilance, on edge, ready for the next remark. And when it was a teacher or someone in authority saying it, it was even worse, because they're the people that teach others, people who other people look up to.

I always had an insecurity, a big dread of the teachers, because of their superiority, and the fact that they were in charge. I was afraid of their reactions, and their not knowing, because obviously if they did react badly, and they're the adult, then what was every-one else going to act like?

I spent my entire teenage years trying to avoid these kinds of moments, gripped with the fear of when the next one might happen. It meant that any kind of self-acceptance or self-worth was beyond me in most aspects of my life, because it could feel as if everything around me was telling me I was not enough. Different meant being of less value.

Things got to a point where I had no self-worth or self-respect. I found it hard to have an opinion about anything, and I constantly doubted myself. In the classroom, I hated having to answer ques-tions, for fear I would get something wrong. If someone criticised my taste in music, I would internalise that, start to believe that what I thought was stupid.

Eventually, I got sick of it. I knew I could feel better, *knew* I could be happy. I had been a happy, much-loved child. I had experienced happiness and certain levels of confidence in my life in the pool. I wanted to change. It didn't happen overnight, and in many ways I'm still a work in progress, and always will be. But this book is my account of how I did that. How I managed to change, to come to love my differences, to feel comfortable in myself. To love myself.

CHAPTER CHALLENGES

Small – Wake up every morning, look in the mirror and say, 'I love you.' Do this every day, for a month, and see if it makes you feel any different.

Medium – Choose a weekly act that will make you feel as if you are looking after yourself, showing yourself love. It could be a long bath, a massage, a meal with a friend, rewatching your favourite movie, reading a book that makes you think, listening to a favourite album while tidying your house. Think of an activity you might suggest to a friend who had been neglecting themselves, and then do that. Something that means you are taking care of yourself because you are a worthwhile person. Make a list in the notebook you're using as you read through this book, of some things you might like to do, then note down how you feel afterwards.

Big – Remember something you used to love doing as a kid but maybe haven't done in some time, and plan it in for this month. It could be going for a cycle, drawing, baking. Something that has no purpose other than that it is an activity you enjoy, which brings you into the moment.

Dear 10-year-old me,

Thank you for being a dreamer. Without your imagination, none of this would have been possible. It's weird how often I think about you. Whenever I'm struggling, lacking motivation, or feel like I'm not enough, I think about you. You were the most carefree, happy kid there was. You used to love spending your summers in the sea and any chance that you got you were always in the water. It was your happy place. It was the place where you were free to be whoever you were. That hasn't changed. The water is still your sanctuary, except sometimes you have a love-hate relationship with it.

I do all of this for you. I want to respect the kid you were. I want to make you proud of how far we've come and all we have achieved. As much as I think about you and as much as I use you as my motivation, I've never fully reflected and appreciated how far we've come.

Remember that gold medal you dreamt of? Well, we eventually got it, except it took a lot longer than you were hoping. If I'm honest, you just weren't ready for it. You always knew deep down what we were capable of, but somewhere along the way, you stopped being so nice to yourself. And we struggled with that for a little bit. But I kept holding on because of you. I kept moving forward. Your happy and carefree life is the reason I believed I was capable of being happy again. Thank you so much for giving me something to hold on to.

I know right now you're starting to notice boys and being brainwashed by Hollywood. You can't wait to fall in love and find your Prince Charming. But a big part of you believes that he won't want you when you meet him because you're different. You can't see anyone like you on the TV or in the movies. So you believe you're unworthy of being loved. I wish I could hold you right now and tell you how wrong you are. You are so loved because you are different and will try to change the world with your difference.

Your difference is your superpower. Please try to keep smiling; I know it's not always easy, but you will be OK, and everything will make sense.

I'm sorry for the mistakes I'm about to make. And I'm sorry for putting you down. But everything happens for a reason, and I promise you I am happy now.

Keep moving forward.

Love you always,
28-year-old you x

two

Water

'Water does not resist.
Water flows. When you
plunge your hand into
it, all you feel is a caress.
Water is not a solid
wall, it will not stop you.
But water always goes
where it wants to go, and
nothing in the end can
stand against it. Water is
patient. Dripping water
wears away a stone.
Remember that, my child.
Remember you are half
water. If you can't go
through an obstacle, go
around it. Water does.'

Margaret Atwood

Even as a small child, before I became a swimmer, I never had any fear in the water. It could be freezing cold, and I'd still be happy out, just floating. I think it's the lack of gravity. I loved the way being in the water took weight off my body. Even though I was a fit young kid, I would still get back pain from the imbalance of the weight of my two arms. If I had to stand for long periods of time, I would begin to feel it in my back, and it would become really painful. I think that's why I loved the water so much.

There's also the fact that swimming is accessible to all. In other sports you might need equipment, but in swimming, you don't need anything fancy, just a hat, goggles and swimsuit.

My earliest memory of being in water is my lessons in the CRC pool in Clontarf on Friday afternoons. My two brothers and sister were already taking lessons, and so my parents' attitude was, 'We'll just throw her in with everyone else and see how she does.' They never saw my disability as an obstacle. So I learned to swim with my siblings and my cousins.

It's funny, even though I loved being in the water, I hated lessons, hated them so much I couldn't wait to be done. I remember we always had cookies afterwards, the ones you would cut from a log of dough before cooking. I loved that part!

In primary school, people would have their birthday parties at the CRC pool, and I loved that too – again, delighted with being in the water, the freedom of playing. I'm the same as an adult. Even now, on a Sunday, the one day I don't train, sometimes I'll just have a shower because I need to be in water.

A water baby

Childhood holidays were mostly in Kilkee in Co. Clare; I'd spend all summer in the sea, swimming, or taking part in surf camp. No fear in the water, ever. I wasn't especially aware of my arm as a child, but in the water, I forgot entirely about being different.

It must have been obvious to others, this comfort and affinity I felt in the water, because I remember my dad asking me if I wanted to go to a swimming competition in Lisburn when I was around seven. The competition was run for people with disabilities by Disability Sport Northern Ireland. My dad learned about it from a newsletter sent out by Reach, an organisation for people with upper limb differences. Most parents learn about Reach from nurses when a baby is born with a limb difference, so I've been a member since birth.

I decided to try it, and in doing so, discovered that while I might not love lessons, I adored racing. It kind of made sense. I was a high-energy child, all giddiness, all go. I think that's why I didn't like lessons so much; I got bored, it felt restrictive. But with racing, all that energy had something to focus on. They say go, and you just go, you just do it.

I had a natural talent for it, and things just kind of spiralled from there. I raced again the following year, there was a cup that you could win, and I won.

That's how it started.

I started doing lane swimming, and it got to the point where it became obvious this had potential to go somewhere. That I could become a swimmer. To do that, I would need to swim more than I already was.

I think now part of it was the ADHD energy, the buzz, the constant hum; it was a way of channelling it. I was only diagnosed with ADHD after Tokyo. With the diagnosis, a lot of things suddenly made sense. I have always been quite flustered, over-whelmed, very poorly organised, very messy, but I had always put it down to just being tired and stuff. Because of swimming, which took up so much energy, I kind of always had an excuse for the way I was. In college and school, I always felt like something was missing; I didn't understand how everyone else knew what was going on and I didn't. But I always put it down to just being tired because of training.

After Tokyo, when I came home, I was just so overwhelmed by it all. I had been given loads of lovely gifts, people had sent so much post, so many requests were coming in. I think that's probably overwhelming for anyone, but I certainly just wasn't managing it very well, and I happened to say it to my psych, that I thought maybe there was something else going on here. She ran through a general checklist, and then referred me to a specialist.

When I got an appointment with a specialist a few months later, tests showed I did have ADHD. I struggled a lot in the beginning with the diagnosis, because I just didn't believe it. I felt, *how have I gone this long without knowing, and how has no one ever picked up on it?*

I just kept saying they were wrong. It took me a long time to ... not *accept* it, but really *believe* it. But once I started to really lean into my diagnosis, it actually took a lot of pressure off me. I was a lot less hard on myself. It's not that I would use it as an excuse, but it helped me to make sense of myself in ways, and helped me to be kinder to myself. I cut myself a lot more slack.

Now, if I'm struggling with my house being chaotic, or work, or even just learning new things (sound is a really big thing for me as well, and I can get quite overwhelmed by it), just knowing what my triggers are, knowing why I'm finding things challenging, knowing specifically what I'm like, and how to manage that, has really helped.

Because I was being really hard on myself. I couldn't understand why I was incapable of doing really simple things that everyone in the world seemed to be able to do. When I got my diagnosis, it felt like, *Oh, OK, this is how it is, I might need a little bit of help here, I might need to outsource sometimes, or just let people know that it might be a bit chaotic, and that's OK.*

When I'm making new friends I tend to try to bring up that I have ADHD. I almost feel I need to blurt it out straight away. I can sometimes feel afraid that someone might not accept me or be mean to me about the symptoms I have. I was really, really insecure about these symptoms, possibly because people I had been with in the past, or friends in the past, had been mean about how messy I am, or how chaotic I am. Or they had no patience with how hyper I can get. I don't want new people to think I am just being annoying, or I'm being lazy. I feel now in sport I was called lazy a lot because of my ADHD.

Early promise

Obviously I began showing promise early on with swimming, and I remember my dad asking me as a kid, 'Is this what you want to do?' And me saying, 'Sure, whatever' – I didn't really know what it meant, or what that decision would entail. It would be many years before I really understood the amount of work and dedication that that decision, that swimming was what I wanted to do, would require.

Obviously sport itself is hard, whatever kind you do. But swimming is probably the hardest sport on young people. Obviously I know rowing is very, very intense, as is cycling. But for swimming, as a teenager you are getting up at four in the morning before school, then spending all day with wet hair, to then go swim for another two hours in the evening. I don't know any other sport that demands that kind of schedule.

I actually enjoyed the early mornings, though; I think it's easier to get up at four in the morning than it is to get up at seven. It's a different energy at that time, there's something about the silence; it's peaceful. Even when I was in college, I would go to bed early and get up at five to finish assignments.

At the time I was beginning to get properly into swimming, Michael Phelps was starting to become a really big deal; there was so much media attention around him and the American team. I think that's one of the reasons why I didn't mind doing the long hours – it just proves the importance of role models. And there were the friendships that I began to make. You're poolside at quarter to five in the morning with a bunch of other 10-, 11-, 12-year-olds, and you're all just really, really giddy. Then you've to get in the water and bond over how you don't want to do something. The coach will call the set and everyone is like, *Ugh* ... but then you get through it with each other. At times the coach is the hero and at times the coach is a villain. You build really special bonds by doing all of this, every morning and evening. You are part of a team. And then you go to school and I guess there's a certain level of pride when you're in school at 9 a.m. and you've already done two hours of work!

This kind of inclusiveness and camaraderie certainly helped as I began to struggle more and more in school. The pool became the place that I couldn't hide. All you have is your swimsuit, your hat and your goggles; there's literally nowhere to hide. And it was somewhere that I was strong, rather than lacking. When I was in the water and I was swimming, all that mattered was what I was doing in that moment. Getting from point A to point B. I could shut off other stuff, be in the moment.

I learned to love my body that way. For all that it could do.

I learned to feel safe in my body and it didn't matter that I had one arm.

I was still able to swim as fast as the girl beside me.

I was still able to do the same things as everyone else.

There was no negativity around my arm when it came to swimming. It was the one and only place where as soon as I walked on poolside, nothing else mattered. I could disconnect from the world and just be present.

Although the water, and being with my friends there, was my safe place, the amount of time and energy swimming demanded was also holding me back from other parts of my life, like socialising with my friends. It was so draining, and then school itself was so draining. Like most teenagers, I was emotional, and I found my energy spread thinly.

Puberty was difficult. As my body changed, all of a sudden I found myself swimming slower than I had before. As female swimmers' bodies get older, the fat in their bodies moves about and you find yourself floating in other places. When your body changes as an athlete, it's very hard to figure out your balance in the water and how to move that new body through the water. It's a time when boys start to get quicker, and girls get slower. Now for the first time, the fact that I had one arm, and the other girls two, started to make a difference in how fast I was compared to them. I needed to be trained in a specific way that acknowledged my difference, but it would be years before that happened.

I began to have mixed feelings about swimming. In some ways I started to fall out of love with it in my early teenage years. When I came home from Beijing, my first Paralympic Games when I was 13, I never spoke about being a Paralympian. At the time, the Paralympics was still establishing itself, and people would often wrongly refer to me as an Olympian, or talk about the Special Olympics.

Other people's confusion compounded matters. The word *Paralympian* was rarely said. So, if ever anyone said I was an Olympian, I'd say, 'I'm not an Olympian,' because I'm not. This would inevitably draw a response along the lines of, 'What do you mean you're not an Olympian? You went to Beijing.' This would then kick off the whole conversation around me being disabled. It felt to me that by acknowledging that I was an athlete, I was acknowledging that I was disabled, and I didn't want to acknowledge that I was disabled. At the time, I was far from becoming comfortable with it. What should have been an achievement was in many ways a source of shame rather than pride.

I was still swimming, still committed to turning up every day. It's not that I didn't want to be there, but I think I was there as much for the social aspect as anything else. I didn't really understand at that age the kind of hard work that was required of a high-performance athlete. I don't think I really could have. I'd gone to Beijing off talent – like, what 13-year-old goes to a Games off hard work? No one. You get there off being talented.

I can see now that I had been exposed to high performance too soon. I often talk about that with my coach today, how I probably never should have gone to Beijing, because mentally I wasn't mature enough for it, and I didn't understand what it really took. It sort of set me up with unrealistic expectations around what I needed to do to achieve my goals in the pool. The levels of work required. And that meant I struggled for years with not improving as I wanted to.

This problem did not get solved between Beijing and London. I wasn't swimming fast. I wasn't really an athlete. Well, I was an athlete, but I didn't have the qualities of a high-performance athlete. I was making all the wrong decisions and I just expected things to be handed to me, because they had been handed to me in terms of getting to Beijing. So I didn't know how to deal with this next level, how to move myself on and make the necessary improvements.

Even though I always wanted to pursue swimming, there was a lot of conflict and struggle in the pool for me during this time. It was not always a good place for me. I still dreamt of the Paralympics and of winning a gold medal, but I just didn't know how to get there. Personally, it was frustrating. And obviously when you swim slowly, your coaches are going to be angry at you. There was often a lot of conflict and no one was willing or able to recognise why things were like this, why I wasn't swimming well. A lot of blame was put on me, even though I was still so young. I remember being regularly screamed at by my coach during this time. Me and my friends would sit together in the showers crying after training, but you still turned up the next day. You always had to turn up.

In terms of coaching, because Paralympic sport was still growing, there was a lack of understanding and education around the difference between coaching typical bodies and disabled bodies. They didn't necessarily understand how to coach *me* properly. I started to get really bad shoulder injuries because I was overusing my arm, and I wasn't doing any rehab or strength conditioning work to help support it. It meant I would often find it really hard to swim and finish a session, because I was in so much pain, and then I'd be screamed at. The only people you could talk to were your teammates. We were all going through it together, so there was a sense of camaraderie.

I also think there is a difference between the old-fashioned tough coaching style and how coaches now understand how to get the best out of their athletes, acknowledging different strengths and weakness, being vulnerable. I think everyone is learning new methods, and gaining a greater depth of understanding.

In 2010, when I was 15, I went to boarding school in the UK for two years. There was a coach there who was one of the coaches for the ParalympicsGB team; he trained athletes who were Paralympians, including a girl I had raced against for many years, who I had never beaten. When he invited me to come train with them in the school, I didn't even think about it – it was a definite yes! It didn't once occur to me that I might not go. By this stage I had been travelling on my own for three years; my dad had stopped coming away as my chaperone when I was 12, so I was very used to it. And I was a teenager, I was excited at the prospect. Around that time, I was watching *Zoey 101*, and she was in boarding school, and *Harry Potter* was huge – the school itself was considered for Hogwarts scenes in the movies. Because of Harry Potter, all kids wanted to do was go to boarding school and leave their families! So I very much romanticised the whole thing, and that made it easier.

I loved it. For the first year, I absolutely was in my element. I made some really great friends, even though I found it hard to socialise with the students who weren't swimmers. (There was a swim school within the school, so loads of the students were swimmers. But then there were other students who just went to the school.) I found it so hard to bond with them, but I loved being in the swimming world.

I loved the coach, and began swimming really well. Finally, training that was tailored specifically to me: it made such a difference. Unfortunately, he took a step back from coaching after my first year, and I struggled with my training then. There were personal problems as well, a bad relationship. My self-worth began to suffer, and I think for a time I became a functioning depressive, just trying to get through.

Pressure to succeed

There had been so much pressure put on me from such a young age to succeed, and I was failing to do so, and floundering, and I couldn't figure out how to change things, or what I needed to do to make it work. I would always hear from the head coaches about the investment that had been made in me. Why wasn't I performing? Why was I doing this? Why wasn't I doing that? Looking back, there was immense pressure but not enough guidance.

I often got told how talented I was. How much potential I had – always talk of potential. There was a pressure in this, a sense of expectation. But also, looking back, I can see there was also a bonus. I believed the talk, believed in my potential. And therefore, from a very young age, I believed that I was capable of doing something. I think that's what has always driven me. In a way, that's why I stayed in the sport and that's how I ended up succeeding eventually.

I just needed to figure out my own way to get there, to fulfil that potential.

I think the way it was handled when I was a child and later a teenager wasn't helpful. I needed to be taught how to manage things. I never was, and instead it was always expected that I should just know what to do. Which I didn't, because I was a kid.

When I was 18, I started working with my coach Dave Malone, who is still my coach today. He competed at four Paralympic Games himself and brought multiple medals home to Ireland. He understood how to train me so I could reach my full potential. He literally started me from scratch, which was what I needed, and gave me permission to be a beginner.

Until then, I had moved clubs several times, and on occasion, some of the coaches I had would just put me in a side lane and make me wear fins while everyone else was doing something else. It felt like I was just filling the time.

Fins are like flippers. Wearing them would ensure that I was the same speed as everyone else. But technically I wasn't training the same system, wasn't getting the same adaptations, or the same level of fitness. I was being given a prop, rather than really developing my unique body. It wasn't training, it was just plodding up and down, and I wasn't getting any faster or any better.

So for much of my time as a teenager, I was in the water out of a feeling that I had to be there. There was a fear in me; if I didn't swim, what would I do? Because there were no other disabled people for me to look up to; the only disabled people I saw were in sport, and I so saw it as my future. Swimming offered me a meaningful future where I could achieve something.

Deep within I knew I was capable. I had goals. But I hadn't yet learned how to properly identify those goals, how to trust my gut instinct, how to speak up for myself, communicate clearly and directly about what I wanted and needed. I always thought I was capable. I just hadn't yet figured out how to get there.

Many times, I would reluctantly turn up. But deep down I always thought I was capable of something. That is what kept me in the water.

CHAPTER CHALLENGES

Small – Drink more water. Simple as that, every day.

Medium – Do something for your body that allows you to feel good about it. Dance around your house to loud music, take up running, go for a swim, or even create an affirmation that reminds you of how proud you are of it.

Big – Think about your community. Are you a member of a group, formal or otherwise, that makes you feel included, people with whom you enjoy a sense of camaraderie? Consider taking something up, or even setting up something yourself, such as a book club, a walking group, a running club; something that puts you with a group of people with a similar interest, with whom you can connect.

three

New
Beginnings

And suddenly you know: it's time to start something new and trust the magic of beginnings.

Meister Eckhart

I have always loved the idea of new beginnings. The fresh start, the possibilities that that brings, the sense of a blank sheet of paper; whatever you want, you can put on it. A new beginning is a time that allows you to get rid of what isn't working, re-examine what you want to change before you actually move into the next phase. To reconsider things, and figure out what you want to achieve.

For me a new beginning always comes out of the ending of something professional or personal. When something ends, a Games, a relationship, school, I always feel so liberated from it, whether it was a good *or* a bad experience. It's like – *OK, now I can let go of it.*

Because I'm quite an emotional person, I will deeply invest my emotions into something. So when it's over, it's nearly a relief in ways. There can be a period of mourning; in the case of a Games, it can feel quite sad because I have spent four years of my life training for something that happens in a very brief period, and then it's just gone and I have to get onto the next thing. But I put it down and move on.

When something ends, with that ending go all the mistakes that I have made. Moving on to something new, I just take the lessons I've learned from the past, to put into whatever it is I'm doing next. I find that so exciting, this clean slate. You've not yet made any mistakes; you've not fucked up yet. You can literally be anyone you want to be.

Ask yourself what your new beginning could be. Maybe you have picked up this book in January – the start of the new year is a perfect example. But it needn't be so obvious. It could be something much more personal to you. Beginning a new job. Ending a relationship. Just simply deciding you want to make some changes, and with that, ditching old habits, ending ways of behaviour that are not working for you.

A lot of my new beginnings come about because of sport. Your season ends, and no one else really remembers you had a bad one. They only remember your good seasons. Or the good race that you had. So each season is a new beginning, a fresh chance. It's about giving yourself permission to be excited and to think about what can come next.

**It is never too late to allow yourself
a new beginning.**

Rolling up my sleeve

After school, I chose to study culinary entrepreneurship in DIT. It was also at this point that I decided college was going to be my new beginning in my personal life, that I was going to try something new. I had become so sick and tired of feeling unhappy, I felt I had to try something different. If I couldn't yet feel good about myself, I was going to fake it instead.

So I decided that on the first day of college, I was going to roll up my sleeve and embrace who I was. Create a fresh start for myself, show everyone my true self from day one. No more hiding. And that's what I did.

This was a huge deal for me. Even though it was still warm in Dublin that day, the end of the summer, I wore a shirt with sleeves just in case I needed the coverage.

The prospect of what I was about to do felt terrifying. I had by now spent years trying to conceal my arm, keep my disability, and therefore my difference, under the radar, everywhere but in the pool. There were people I had sat with every day for a year in the Institute of Education who had no idea I had one arm.

I was intensely aware as I approached the Cathal Brugha Street building that my arm was not covered up as it usually would be. Even though I had passed the building countless times on my way into town from Clontarf, where I grew up, I couldn't find the entrance. As I was searching for the front door, a girl approached. She introduced herself as Sinéad; she was studying the same course as me. I didn't think she noticed my arm straight away, and we entered, meeting another girl, Shauna, also on our course, on the stairs. A good start.

In the classroom, I ended up sitting beside a guy called Adam. As we chatted, I told him I was a swimmer. It turned out he knew another Paralympian, and as we talked, I felt an invisible safety net slowly begin to stretch out beneath me. I started to relax. Maybe this might be OK? I survived the day, even getting through my chair breaking, and momentarily being the centre of the class's attention. It was fine, everyone laughed, I laughed. It was a normal thing that could happen to anyone in college. My sleeve stayed rolled up.

On the second day, our lecturer was giving a demonstration on passing knives safely. He chose me to be a part of it, in front of the entire class. To do it as he showed us, you needed to have two hands. I knew immediately I would not be able to repeat what he had done, so I did it my own way. It was embarrassing, and I remember just wanting it to be over. Afterwards, I stayed back to explain that I might need to do certain things differently.

'I'm just going to tell the lecturer that I have one arm,' I told Sinéad and Shauna, as everyone began to leave the room. I automatically felt safe with these two girls, and when I left the classroom after talking to my lecturer, they were still there, waiting for me.

Slowly, as the term progressed, my confidence started to build. I began to notice that my thoughts were just that: thoughts, not real. And that yes, people would stare, but then they would move on.

How to stop hiding

The more I stopped hiding, and instead spoke up about who I was, the easier it became. I had spent seven years of my life hiding under coats and hoodies, terrified of anyone seeing who I really was, and what their reactions might be. Now, in the first year of my course, I began to let go of the person I had been throughout my secondary school years. To shed some of the fears that had kept me trapped, held back.

Gradually I began to realise that the assumptions I had made in my head were not necessarily true. I had automatically assumed Adam did not know anyone with a disability; in fact *I* was already judging *him*, by assuming he would judge me. I could have missed out on his friendship, because of my mistaken assumption about his beliefs and experiences.

Maybe my assumption that no one would understand me had been holding me back?

With college, I was faced with the chance of a new beginning, and I grabbed it. There was a liberation to it; where in school being different from the pack had felt terrifying, now it felt like you could do, or be, anything, and no one would give a damn. I began to feel free.

As first year progressed, *I began to notice how light I felt, how much happier I was becoming in myself.* When we went out, I no longer felt the need to wear long sleeves to conceal myself. My new beginning was working, and things were changing for me.

Letting go isn't always easy and it is not always positive. Yes, moving from secondary school to college was largely a good experience, but there have been other new beginnings which were more mixed. It's important to honour that, to acknowledge all the emotions involved as you move from one phase of your life to another. It's rarely black and white. But a new beginning is always a chance for change.

CHAPTER CHALLENGES

Small – Instigate small changes. Make a list of tiny things you could do differently that might help reset your momentum. Think of one thing you could do each day that would make you feel good. It could be as small as waking up earlier, or planning your outfit the night before, so your morning is not rushed. Try using your notebook to write down all of the things you need to do the next day and get them out of your head.

Medium – Who are the people in your life with whom it feels safe to be yourself? Notice how you feel around them and try to spend more time with them. Conversely, who are the people with whom you do not feel safe enough to be yourself? It might be time to start focusing on only populating your life with the former.

Big – Think of something currently in your life that is not serving you. Try to be open-minded when you do this, examining all aspects of your life: habits, people, work, activities, beliefs. What is holding you back? What would you like to leave behind? How can you push yourself out of your comfort zone? It might seem scary at first – rolling up my sleeve was initially terrifying – but each time you do it, it will become easier. Keep a record in your notebook of how you feel trying this new thing, and note the changes. Does it get easier, do you become less fearful?

four

Alone

Solitude helps you find peace, peace helps you find happiness.

Anon

Rolling up my sleeve was the first step to building up my confidence, which was the missing piece in my racing all along. Now, I like to spend the day of a big race on my own, focusing on my mental state, responsible only for myself, my thoughts and actions. I'm happy in my own company on those days.

When I woke up that morning in Tokyo, I felt so ready. This was my first race of the Tokyo Games, my main event, and it was day two.

The Games had originally been scheduled to take place in 2020, but because of Covid-19, they had been pushed back to 2021. Still, the stadium was going to be empty; my family had bought tickets, hoping they would be able to come over, but they would watch me from their living room in Clontarf, with neighbours out on the street, not allowed into the house. My team were the only supporters I had in the stands cheering me on.

Each room in the athletes' village is small, bare, with white walls. There's a tiny little wardrobe which has no door. Because I've always been – at various stages throughout my swimming career – either the only girl under 18, or the only girl over 18, I've always had my own room. Because Tokyo was aiming to be the most sustainable Games ever, everything was recycled. The frame of my bed in the athletes' village was made of cardboard, the mattress out of tiny bits of plastic. I was so focused I had convinced myself I was comfortable in order to sleep, but the minute I finished racing, I found it hard to sleep in that bed!

Every Games has a duvet cover you get to keep, with the dates and logos of the Games on it, except for Beijing for some reason. I have a London 2012 duvet, a Rio duvet and now I have a Tokyo one too. I've always thought I'll have as many kids as I have duvet covers, and they can each have one. Paris will be my fifth Games; thank God Beijing didn't have any!

The night before a race I make out my plan. You have to be in the check-in call room area 15 minutes beforehand, but as someone who's paranoid, I like to get there 20 minutes beforehand, because if you're even a second after the 15-minute mark you're disqualified; it can be quite stressful. I note down all the times I need to be places, check-in, the time needed to get into my racing suit, however long I need to warm-up, how long it will take me to get there. All are allotted for.

I'm on my own for all of this; I quite like being alone and in my own head. I've worked on my mental strength so much now that, where this might have felt daunting in previous years, now it's my comfort zone. I don't want any distractions.

Focus on the moment

The night before I'll screenshot my schedule and send it to the support staff, so they know what's going on and where I'll be at various times. My coaches are always at the pool but only step in when I need a time taken during my warm-up, or help or opinions on something. I want to just focus all my energy in my head; I don't see the point in making small talk in those hours. I'm responsible for myself at that moment, and I'm going to look after that energy and not hang around, manage or spend time with others. I have my headphones on, head down, I'm completely focused.

I don't pack my bag the night before because I always feel like I'm going to forget something if I do that, so I do it after I wake up. I have breakfast on my own, and then I get the transport from the village to the pool by myself. When I get to the pool, I go to the team area where we do our stretching and stuff. I remember in London 2012, I had a teammate who went on to win a gold medal. I knew beforehand he was going to achieve a gold, not especially because of anything he was doing in the pool, but just the way he held himself, the way he was and his presence. After I'd won my gold medal, Dave, my coach, told me that another of my team-mates had said the same thing to him about me: 'Ellen is going to win a gold medal.' He could see it in the way I was that morning.

I have a really nice relationship with one of the girls that I race against. She's Canadian. We're the closest thing to what you would call rivals – we're always leapfrogging each other. In Rio she won gold, and I won bronze, and then I won gold in Tokyo. Who knows what's going to happen in Paris between the two of us?

I've been racing her since 2007, so we've really grown up together. In the call room we kind of have an unspoken ritual; she'll help me put my racing suit on and I'll help her put her hat on. I'll just walk up to her, and she'll know straight away. I don't even have to speak to her. She'll just fix my straps and I'll fix her hat. This is probably the most interaction I have with someone before my race.

After stretching, I do my swim warm-up. On this occasion the girl I was racing against for first place, who eventually came second, got in the lane with me. I remember thinking that was a bit weird. Every other lane was empty. Maybe she was trying to psych me out. I didn't care: I was so focused on what I was doing that it wouldn't have even dawned on me to play mind games with someone.

A heat swim, which comes after the warm-up, is always a fun one because you have all this energy that you kind of need to get out of your system. For the heat, we were side-by-side and I beat her in the heat as well. But my turn was really bad, and I knew I could improve on that. The purpose of the heat, beyond the fact that the eight fastest make it to the final, is that you can watch it back and see what you could improve on for the final.

It's an opportunity to kind of shake the cobwebs off, make all the mistakes in the heat. After a couple of minutes with the media, I did my swim down, cooling off to get all the lactate out of my body and recover for the final. And then I went back to the village for about five or six hours, had food and a nap. Right up to the moment I dive into the pool on a big race day, I like to be on my own, that to me is how I can stay focused and in the moment. It's not a scary place for me to be, alone in my mind.

A room of my own

The first time I stayed in a room on my own at a training camp I was twelve, in Beijing the year before the 2008 Games. At home, secondary school was beginning, my classmates were getting to grips with new teachers and new friends, but here I was, surrounded mostly by adults and missing the first week of first year, when everyone was getting to know everyone, beginning to get their bearings.

At the Beijing Games the following year, where I would place sixth in the 100m breaststroke, and at the age of 13 become Ireland's youngest Paralympian athlete, the next girl up in age on our team was 18 (the second youngest person, a boy on our team, was 14).

Being alone at swim camp even at the age of 12 didn't faze me at all. I loved it. Secondary school was a different matter. In the face of so much change – new teachers, new classmates, new subjects – I began to feel anxious and afraid. It started to feel like the only way for me to exist safely was, as much as I could, to essentially hide. To be smaller, less than I could be. Blend in and try to conceal my difference, something as a teenager I began to feel much more than I had in primary school. In fact, rather than feeling one of the crowd, I felt increasingly isolated; it was a form of being alone I didn't enjoy.

On shopping trips, I would seek out the biggest jumpers I could find, anything that would conceal my body. Socially, I became extremely shy around friends. Looking back, I feel like I lost my voice, the more self-conscious I became.

My arm meant I felt different, the worst possible thing at that age; no teenager wants to stand out.

The sense of being different in a negative way had really started to kick in the summer before I started first year, when we had gone on a family holiday to Florida. One day at the beach I went on my own to the bathrooms. The tap was the kind that needs to be held down continuously to get the water to run, not one-hand friendly. A woman came in as I was trying to figure things out. 'Don't worry about that,' she said, starting to help me. 'We get shark attacks all the time around here, so we see people without limbs regularly.'

Until then, I hadn't been especially self-conscious about my arm, but suddenly in that moment, something clicked. She had noticed me because I was different. The incident jolted me out of my own safe world and I started to become aware of the reactions of those around me. I began to realise others were noticing my difference too.

Adults' reactions were harder to deal with than kids'. Kids might stare for a moment, but then the next they would be completely distracted. A grown man staring was an entirely different matter. Understandably, it made me feel very uncomfortable. It was then that I began to conceal myself, to hide my arm; in pictures from that holiday, I stand with my two arms resting behind my back. I had figured out that you could see two elbows, but nothing else, and so it just looked as if two hands were behind my back. Or I'd always have my sleeve down, so you couldn't see where my arm ended.

As I said earlier, I've got to the point in my life where I really enjoy time on my own. If my training gets cancelled last minute, I'm just as likely not to tell anyone, and instead use the opportunity to spend some time at home alone, enjoying my own company. But in my early teenage years I started to feel alone, and not in a good way. I was lonely.

It didn't help that it felt as if there was no one I could confide in, no one in my world who seemed to have gone through something similar and would therefore be a safe person to talk to because they would understand. There was no one in the world around me, or the wider media world, who physically matched me. I assumed no one would understand. I never told anyone about the shark comment. Instead, I began internalising a lot of how I felt about my arm, and became more and more distant from those around me. This only served to make me feel more different from everyone else. It was like a never-ending cycle.

As my swimming career progressed I became more used to being around adults. The Games aren't really a place for children – they are a job, something that adults do. With my place on the team came the expectation that I would behave like an adult. And even when I was a young teenager, I was treated like an adult.

After Beijing, a lot of athletes on our team retired, and suddenly I was the only girl on a team of boys. I began to struggle to make friends with girls; so much of my time was spent with my male teammates or older women in the swimming world. When it came to girls my age, I found it hard to interact with them, to find a common ground. I found it easier to talk to the guys at swimming.

In my all-girls school I did have friends, but I never really felt like I fit in. Without the instant shared interest that sport provides, I struggled to make connections. At the same time, as I moved into my teenage years, I was becoming more and more insecure about my arm, but still telling no one about how I felt, going through it on my own.

I had always felt quite safe as a kid. I'd never been bullied, and I loved my primary school. On the day of graduation, I was inconsolable, so sad to be leaving. I think part of it was because I felt so at home. As a kid, we never moved. I always stayed in the same house: I think I moved bedroom once and it broke my heart. I was so good at routine and familiarity and knowing what was happening. And the thought of having to go where there was going to be loads of new people really scared me – even though the majority of people in my primary school were going to the same secondary school, so I was going to be with a certain number of familiar kids. It was like a switch went off in my head, that even the girls who I grew up with, and the girls from other classes in primary school, who clearly would have known that I had one arm, were automatically going to now judge me and stare at me. I was just so afraid of the stares. Afraid of not being worthy.

As time went on, I became really bad at standing up for myself, I hated conflict. Whenever I got into fights with friends or anything, I'd automatically be the first to apologise, and there would nearly be a desperation in me to fix the problem, because I was so afraid of being abandoned. I don't know where that came from. But because of that, I started to allow myself to be disrespected by others in the name of kind of keeping the peace. It meant I wasn't respecting myself.

The older I got, the worse it became; I grew more silent and uncomfortable in social situations, especially when it came to meeting new people; at times I would barely say a word. Even if someone were to initiate a conversation with me, I would often find an excuse to end it as quickly as possible, giving such short answers that the conversation simply couldn't continue. The giddy, bubbly child who loved to run around and play was disappearing.

I was afraid of authority, afraid of my coaches, my teachers. I just wanted to keep the peace, slip through life unnoticed, not stand out. To do that, I made myself small, became a people-pleaser, agreed with others even when I actually thought or felt otherwise, anything to avoid drawing attention to myself. My mental strength was non-existent.

It even began to affect how I performed in the pool. I didn't know how to relax and trust myself when it came to racing. I was so good at negative self-talk that I was totally lacking in courage and self-belief, instead blaming myself for never doing well enough, for never achieving my potential. Berating myself constantly, stuck in a cycle that mentally dragged me down.

It got to the point where my self-confidence was so low, I began to believe that my voice didn't matter anymore. The way I saw it was that my disability made me less of a person. Being different made me less of a person. When you're a teenager, everyone is trying to look the same. And I couldn't; no matter how hard I tried, I was never going to look like everyone else. Back then, I couldn't possibly conceive of difference as something wonderful, something that I would come to consider my superpower, a thing to lean into. That it would become one of the things about myself that I was most proud of, which made me unforgettable in a really good way, and paved the way for so many opportunities and achievements.

Finding a safe space

Instead, back then, I felt entirely unworthy, that even my thoughts and opinions were less valuable than those of my peers. I was completely unable to stand up for myself. Even still today, I would struggle with conflict, but back then, people-pleasing was my number one driving force. *Just try to keep the peace.* All this fear and worry got in the way of making true connections, and I became more and more isolated and lonely.

There *was* one place, beyond my family, where I could always be entirely myself, a group of people with whom I felt no need to hide or be silent. Being in the pool, swimming and with my teammates, was mostly a place where I felt safe, at ease, comfortable in myself.

I could be this mute, introverted person everywhere else in my world, and then go to swimming and spend the time laughing and feeling happy. I could never hide my arm when I was swimming, but I didn't feel the need to. I just had to focus on doing what I needed to do, and, for the most part, I was treated the same as everyone else.

The pool was also the place where I could be alone but in a good way. In the call room lining up before a race, it can be pretty silent; you're essentially alone with your thoughts, maybe some music. It's a high-pressure, uncomfortable situation, and you have to handle it on your own. It forces you to trust yourself, to really believe in yourself. And that needs to come from within;

there is no one else there in that moment to give that to you, you are all you have to rely on. It forces you to become comfortable with being alone.

I could face being alone in the pool, in fact I welcomed it; it was an entirely different type of solitariness from that which I experienced in school and my social life. I could be myself, comfortable, no need to hide, not isolated. In the pool I typically felt good about myself, strong. Even though I was with a team, I might spend a total of ten minutes of a two-hour session talking to people. Other than that, it is a lot of time alone in your head, up and back, up and back. So swimming for me was the unscary part of being alone.

Alone and strong. Alone, but also surrounded, for the most part, included.

But everywhere else in my life, I struggled. Tried to hide within the crowd, to conceal my differences. I desperately tried to be a part of the groups of friends, while in fact always feeling like an outsider.

Striking out on my own

When I started college at 19 I moved out of my family home. I think I had to move out because I already felt like an adult. I always had. Since Beijing, I had always been the youngest person on the team. So I had spent a lot of time alone, and I became independent very young. Then later I went to boarding school, I was living away from home, and obviously there were rules and stuff in boarding school, but you still got a level of independence that you wouldn't have if you were still living at home.

Then when I came home from boarding school, I found it so hard having to be back in my family home. My mum and dad would do anything for me. And they *have* done *everything* for me; I wouldn't have had the career I have had without them. But it got to a point where I felt, *if I'm going to do this, I have to do this on my own. I don't want to rely on other people because if I don't succeed, I'll blame them. Whereas, if I don't succeed and I've done it all myself, at least I will know I did everything I could.* I didn't want to be able to blame people. I wanted to take that away, and rely on myself alone. So when I turned 19, I moved out. I was focusing on Rio, in college, and I loved the independence of it all.

Really, by that stage, I was already used to independence, because even aside from boarding school, I had travelled so much without my family. My parents of course weren't thrilled. Because I'd been away so much, and I had just only been home two years from boarding school, I think my mam just missed me and didn't want me to grow up, wanted more time with me at home.

I moved into an apartment in Blanchardstown, where I was sharing with my landlady. She had a spare room and she wanted to fill it. She was 35. I couldn't share with a normal student because even in college, I had an early bedtime! I had to train in the mornings.

My early mornings then would be 8 a.m., a little later than in school. But I would still need to get my sleep. And I would still need to be able to know that I could come home to a quiet house. It's so funny when you're on Daft as a 19-year-old emailing the landlady who's in her thirties, a professional who works 9 to 5, Monday to Friday, and you're like, 'Hi, I'm a college student. Can I move into your house?' And you have to explain, 'No, I'm an athlete. I live a very boring life. It will be almost like I'm not there.' And it was.

I had spent years being quite introverted. When I was going through my whole phase of hiding my arm and being really insecure, it was like I had tried my best to be present, but also invisible. So I didn't have great social skills. Meeting new people was really, really difficult for me.

Even now I would still kind of struggle a little bit when I meet new people. I don't know if that's because I was so incapable of social interactions when I was younger, and it's the remains of that, or if it's because I've kind of been in the bubble of sport for so long that I don't know how to come up with other topics of conversation.

Cat lady

I had a near inability to talk in social situations. I'd be just sitting there, alarms blaring, trying to think of things to say. So when I first moved into that apartment, my landlady was so nice, but she would eat her dinner in the kitchen and I'd be in the sitting room, or if she was in the sitting room, I'd be in the kitchen – we never spent any time together.

After about a year and a half, she wanted to move her boyfriend in. So I moved out, into a very similar situation in a house in Ongar. The landlady worked nights. I'd be out all day and then I'd be asleep or I'd be quiet. We just had such different schedules that it was always just one of us in the house. I did love being on my own, but I did feel very lonely. I don't think I was quite ready then for living alone, like I am now.

She had a cat, though. My first experience of pets as a child was my cat, Lucky, when I was a kid. My brothers are two years older than me, and they're twins, so they have each other. And then my sister is seven years older than me; she didn't really want to hang around with me at all, so my best friend in the house was my cat. There's a little step in my parents' back garden. I would pretend it was a stage, and I'd perform in front of Lucky the cat. I had a really big connection with cats for so long, I was kind of a cat lady. But then my parents got a dog, Glenn, and now I have two dogs.

Animals make you feel less lonely. They kind of fill the void. They're there for you, they're creatures that you can love unconditionally without any expectation. During lockdown, I moved into an apartment on my own, to avoid getting sick and to help prevent my teammates getting sick. I had a lot more time, and that's when I got Denny, my first dog.

I always tell him he's the love of my life. Denny doesn't ever stray too far from me. Raffa, my other dog, runs around but Denny is always close to my side. When I went through a break-up,

Denny wouldn't let me sleep alone. Any time I was crying, he would come over to me, any time I was upset he would come close. He just knows when I'm down and when I need a little bit of extra love. Your pet is going to love you no matter what. And all they ask in return is to be fed and walked a little.

Now I can see that cultivating the ability to be alone is really important, but it can be scary, and it's easy to try to avoid being on your own instead. I think like everything, when you're trying to push yourself outside of your comfort zone, a kind of gradual exposure therapy works. Keep pushing yourself to try whatever it is, in this case, doing things on your own, spending time alone. It will gradually get easier. School, college, work, all provide methods that help us avoid it. For me, I think I used relationships as a way to avoid it.

I can see now that I was searching for self-acceptance in other people. Instead of ever giving myself a chance to be fully alone and open to what that might bring, the confidence it might give rise to, the self-knowledge, even maybe self-acceptance, I would lose myself in a relationship then, inevitably, yet again become very unhappy because I wasn't being given what I needed. Find myself not being treated well, but put up with it because I felt as if I wasn't worthy of better. Of course I would have been better off alone, but it can take time to realise that, to know that you are enough in yourself.

I did eventually get to the point where I had reached a *certain* acceptance about my arm and my body, but I still hadn't *fully* accepted myself. It meant I was choosing the wrong people in relationships all the time, nearly as an act of self-harm, because I didn't feel good enough. I would choose people who weren't good enough for me, because I felt at least they would stay. I never had a baseline standard of respect that I expected for myself.

Deep down I had convinced myself that I would be properly happy when I met someone. The potential source of happiness was always located within someone else, never me. In a new relationship, I would try to rush things, want us to quickly become boyfriend and girlfriend, without really stopping to question whether I was really happy, was I getting what I needed? There was a big relationship in my twenties: we lived together, shared a dog, I finally thought I had reached the point of having figured things out. That this was it.

And then it ended.

I was blindsided when that relationship fell apart. But in the aftermath, I came to realise that I hadn't remotely figured stuff out yet, and I knew I needed to do things differently. I had to get comfortable with being on my own.

Even if there had been someone to talk to about how I was feeling when I was a teenager, finding understanding in someone else wasn't going to create the change. Change had to come from within.

It never occurred to me to share all of this with anyone, to tell anyone how I was feeling. I think I would have worried that no one would understand. That I might have been belittled for my insecurities. If this *had* happened, it would have made everything so much worse, sent me back into my shell forever more. I can see now that maybe these fears were in my own head in part. Either way, it was important for me to go on this journey alone.

Turning point

The ability to change had to come from me deciding that I'd had enough of feeling like this, and that's exactly what happened. To put it bluntly, I got to the point where I had just had enough of my own crap! I thought, *this is shit, this isn't who I am.*

I knew that I could be happy. I knew what that felt like, and I knew what it felt like to be comfortable in my own skin, so I knew both were possible for me. In the pool, it is just me, my goggles, my swimsuit. Nothing to hide, all differences on show, and I had always felt comfortable.

The word *alone* can be a daunting word, but I think it's an important word to be comfortable with. It's only by being alone that you really have the space to think and reflect and figure out what it is you want. Figure out your own voice.

For me, now, being alone is when the magic happens. There are no distractions, no room to hide. This is the time when I can really grow.

When you take that deep breath, push through the fear of it, or the urge to run away and hide from yourself, and instead sit alone with yourself, you begin to realise, *this isn't who I am*.

On your own, you can ask yourself:

Who am I?

What do I want?

Who do I want to be?

Through sport I've been on my own a lot. And it has been hard at times. But I really value it, and I consider myself very lucky to have had this time. It helped me to realise that there's so much strength and value in being able to do whatever you want, whenever you want. More recently, I've grown into being comfortable with being alone, not just in the pool, but in my personal life, and what I learned in my sport helped me to get to that. It's wild to me, looking back on what I used to be like. It makes me so sad, because it wasn't living, it wasn't happiness at all. Now, I can just do what I want on my own, and it doesn't bother me. That's because I found comfort in my own company. I know this might sound strange, because being human is all about connection, and finding other humans to connect with, but I think you need to build your base within yourself first.

Control what you can

Succeeding in sport always goes back to looking at what is in your control. What you can control is up to you. No matter how much you share with other people, at the end of the day you're the one who has control over the things that will make you stronger, in the pool, or in life in general. So I guess, in my journey of self-acceptance, that was what was in my control; choosing to be alone.

I thought I had it sorted. But when the big relationship broke up, I realised that my foundation was him, not myself. When it all came crumbling down, I felt so alone, in a bad way, that I knew I needed to learn how to feel alone in a good way.

No matter how much I liked anyone else, it was really important to me to build my own foundation before I began anything new. Even though I'm now in a relationship, I'm still doing that; it's an ongoing project, learning how to maintain my boundaries, not losing myself in this relationship.

I knew I needed to have the ability to be comfortably on my own and to learn how to properly look after myself. Because if your foundation is other people, what happens when they are not there? You fall apart. Share experiences with people, of course. Connect, find your people who understand you and your experiences. But first have a solid foundation within, beyond all of that, so that if things do go wrong, you know how to look after yourself, and you are enough, just you.

With the ending of that big relationship, I finally had to really face how uncomfortable I was with being alone. I had to face how much of myself I had lost. That was hard to sit with, but ultimately life changing.

Ask yourself: What are you hiding from?

The more you do this, the more you face the pain, the difficult stuff you have been running from, and instead sit with yourself alone, the easier it gets. The dark stuff has less of a hold on you, and you will feel euphoric after facing up to it. Let it out, in whatever messy way it comes, as often as needed.

Each time you do this, it becomes a less painful process. It also gets less scary. Confronting it makes it smaller, gives it less of an opportunity to creep up on you and to catch you off guard. In fact, deciding to confront whatever it is that you have been avoiding sitting alone with, deciding to stop denying whatever stuff you are carrying for the first time, is usually the scariest part, rather than the actual stuff you have been avoiding dealing with.

I knew I could do this, because in the pool I was alone, so I knew I had the mental strength to face whatever I needed to in other aspects of my life, because in swimming I had done that.

In sport, as with anything physical, a lot of it is about mental strength more than anything else. If you're able to overcome or get through something hard, like a training session, you get so much more confidence in your own abilities. And your mind becomes stronger, along with your body.

Find that thing that allows you to get comfortable being on your own. It doesn't have to be sport. It could be a hobby – sewing or drawing – I'm just not artistic in the slightest! Something that allows you to be by yourself. Where you're not influenced by anything that is going on around you. Something that gets you into a flow state. For me, it can be cleaning; I sometimes feel I make a mess just to clean!

After that big break-up, I promised my oldest friend that I would be single for a year. She's met all of my exes, seen it all. And for a time I was. Then she called me one day for a catch-up.

'What's new?' she asked; she lives abroad and we like to catch up regularly. There was a silence. 'You have a boyfriend, don't you?'

'I'm so sorry,' I said, laughing. 'You're going to be so disappointed in me … I swear this time it's different.'

And it is.

The relationship I'm in now, I explained that I needed to continue learning how to be on my own. Previously, I would have wanted to get the label of being boyfriend–girlfriend nailed down quickly. But this relationship has happened at a much slower pace. Now, I prioritise me time, rather than rushing after *us* constantly. I know I still need to get stuff out of my system. To figure out how to be happy. He knows that I'm still figuring things out, but he is understanding and patient and gives me that space. I have never had that before.

I know my boundaries. I'm focusing on myself, rather than plunging in and losing myself in the relationship.

In relationships, there are compromises that you're going to have to make, but that doesn't mean you have to *lose* yourself in the compromise. You have to find someone who's also willing to make those compromises and sacrifices. There has to be balance. I don't think I had ever found that balance previously. I know now that I need to use what makes me happy as my guiding compass, rather than what makes the other person happy, and then chase that. I need to know who I am and to create my solid base within myself. I have learned to be alone.

CHAPTER CHALLENGES

Small – Create a morning or evening routine which allows you 15 minutes to yourself. It might be a short act of self-care every evening, a quick shower, writing in a journal, meditation, deep breathing. If 15 minutes initially seems dauntingly long, start with 5. Just a quick break away from it all, on your own. Something that helps you to start getting comfortable with time on your own. See if you start to look forward to this small break, maybe even gravitate towards it.

Medium – Pick one activity to do alone, once a week. A walk, a trip to the cinema, a visit to a coffee shop, even a meal. Ideally, something that takes you slightly out of your comfort zone; even gently, push out the boundaries of what you are comfortable doing alone.

Big – Stand in front of a mirror and consider yourself. Take some time with this. Really think about every aspect of your life. Is there anything you are hiding from? Something you are not admitting to? Are there parts of your life you would like to change? Ask yourself, is this the life you want? If the answer is no, then it's your responsibility to figure it out, and your responsibility alone.

This might feel scary at first, but allow the feelings of fear to come, and see what answers lie beyond. Use your notebook to write down whatever comes to your mind. See what this act sparks off.

Dear 15-year-old me,

I hardly recognise you. You're a little bit lost right now. You're angry and frustrated, and you don't understand why. You feel immense pressure, and you're so tired. All the time. You're also making some foolish decisions, but it's OK ... I forgive you.

You make me feel so sad. I know all you care about right now is feeling loved and swimming fast. But you're not swimming fast, and you are allowing people to treat you badly because you're so desperate to be loved. You're giving certain people all you have to offer, and you have nothing left for yourself. I wish you could love yourself first before you try to love someone else, because if you did, you wouldn't be treated the way you are right now. You would be able to find people worthy of your love. It isn't your fault. You just choose to always see the good in people. But sometimes, there is more bad than good, and you are worthy of greatness.

It's also not your fault that you're swimming slowly. You were thrown into the deep end too soon. You needed to learn how to be an athlete. You need to learn how to work hard. The next few years are going to be rough. Your anger will grow, and your loneliness will grow. But you will get a new beginning soon. And all that you are going through right now is a learning opportunity. It sucks, but life is your greatest teacher.

I know you feel incredibly ashamed of your body and the fact that you are so different. This feeling is heavy, and you will carry it for a couple more years. It makes me sad that you want to be like everyone else because I wouldn't change my body for anything. We figured it out, though. We get half-price nails, and we get to skip the queue at Disneyland. Having one hand is a good thing.

I wish I could tell you to stop trying to grow up. You are 15 years old; you are a baby. I wish people could allow you to be a child because that is precisely what you are. Adulthood isn't as exciting as it may seem. But it is what it is, and the only thing I can say to you is that I forgive you, and none of this was ever your fault.

I love you,
28-year-old you x

five

Goals

Set goals so high
that they demand
an entirely different
version of you.

Ebonee Davis

I kind of feel like goals are essential to life. I don't know how you can really get any satisfaction without having a goal, even if it's as small as 'I'm going to get up at this time in the morning.' The small sense of accomplishment that comes from achieving even tiny goals builds momentum.

I really struggled with my training for my last World Championship. My body was drained, and I wasn't making the kind of progress I wanted to. It was frustrating and upsetting, not meeting the goals I had set myself. When this happens, it can be easy sometimes to blame everyone else. But in the end, there's a level of responsibility that you have to take yourself. I pulled through, ultimately winning a medal, because I put to use everything I have learned about going back to basics with my goals when it feels like I am struggling to progress.

For almost as long as I can remember, I have lived my life through goals. What those goals are has changed over the years, but they have nearly always been set for me by other people.

I've been trying to figure out what is not working, why I'm not achieving my aims. When this happens, I have to be completely honest with myself: ask what am I doing right, what am I doing wrong? Take responsibility.

Have I really just been going through the motions?

Am I truly emotionally connected to the goal I am trying to achieve?

Were the goals I set realistic or was I being overly ambitious?

Do I need to make changes?

Is my timeline too tight?

Back to basics

After honestly assessing the situation, it's about going back to the basics and starting to rebuild from there.

In these times, it's important to be kind to yourself. First, I need to accept the situation, and not be afraid to say, 'OK, this is where I am right now.' Accept that at this moment, much as I might not like it, this is the actual baseline. It's shit, I hate it, it's not fun, but tomorrow I'm going to be better, and the day after that I'm going to be even better again.

Making tiny steps each day slowly builds momentum. At the end of each week, I can reflect back on all the things I've achieved. At the moment, my daily goals are meeting my calorie and protein targets. When the big goals feel unattainable, it's about setting the little tiny ones that you know are achievable every day. That's where you get your motivation from, because you can see yourself ticking those boxes.

For me, going back to the basics means focusing on the little things that will take me on the path towards my bigger goal. The building blocks from which everything else I want to achieve will come. Checking again, am I eating enough, getting enough sleep, drinking enough water, getting enough rest, doing something every day that feels like self-care?

In the pool, small goals are certain specific technical things I might want to work on every day, or a specific time I want to hit in the set.

GOALS

These are the things which will give me my foundation and stability when I'm struggling with the big goals and beginning to feel overwhelmed and daunted by the task at hand. I need to break it down. And keep reminding myself that as long as I move forward today, tomorrow and each day, then I'm getting better. Monitoring your self-talk when you are getting new goals off the ground is very important.

Once you gain momentum with your small daily goals, confidence starts to build, and a sense of possibility grows. You start another week buoyant with confidence. Week after week, the tiny goals are part of the journey of getting to the big one.

You do not become a champion in a day. A champion is made in the little things they do every day. By living a champion's lifestyle every day. Sometimes I can forget this and sometimes I struggle, because I'm human at the end of the day. But in those moments it's just about going back to the basics of those small, daily goals and reminding myself that this is what it takes. Trying to stay focused in the moment, clocking my daily achievements.

The thing about a goal is, if it is set by someone else, that makes it harder to connect to the outcome you are aiming for, to show up and do what is required. A goal set by someone else doesn't create the emotional attachment you need to achieve it. For that you need to know deep inside why you want this, and it has to have personal meaning for you, not just be something that exists on the surface level, imposed upon you from the outside.

Now, I will only accept goals I have set for myself.

Goals don't always need to be around self-improvement. When I broke up with my ex-boyfriend, one of my goals became spending more time with my friends, because they always made me feel good about myself. When I met Sinéad, my agent, in 2016, she asked me, 'What are your goals?' My goals were to help grow Paralympic sport in Ireland, to help change perception of disability in Ireland. And to do *Dancing with the Stars*.

I wanted to do *Dancing with the Stars* because it was something fun that had nothing to do with swimming. It had all the glamour, all the hair and makeup, the costumes, but it was still a way of exercising, of moving my body. I saw it and thought, *I can do that and that would be so fun*. It wasn't even about being disabled on the show, it was just, *that looks like fun and I want to do that*. So that was why I'd always thought, *I want to do* Dancing with the Stars. When the pandemic happened in 2020 and the show got cancelled, I was devastated, because they had asked me to be on it before and I had always said, 'Not until after Tokyo.'

But I had been so excited at the thought of finally getting to go on. I had always thought, *I'm going to do* Dancing with the Stars *in January 2021*. And then the Games got postponed, the show got cancelled, and I was just like, *it's fucked, it's not coming back, I'm never going to get a chance to do it*. But the day I won gold, Sinéad got a phone call to say that the show was coming back and they wanted me on. It felt like a sign: I had to do it. This was a chance to achieve one of my goals.

Beginners' goals

Goals first entered my life with the first whispers about Beijing, when I was 11. Initially, it was about needing to hit a certain time if I wanted to qualify for the Games. Without realising what it was called, I began using the practise of visualisation. Before a race I would imagine how it would play out. When I was 12, my team-mates and I received a calendar leading up to Beijing, a timeline laying out the training schedule. I knew exactly how the next year was going to go. It was the first time I had seen what a plan for achieving a goal looked like.

In May 2008, weeks before the Games were due to take place, when I was 13, my appendix burst. As I was rushed to hospital in an ambulance, all I could think was *I'm not going to get to Beijing now.*

After surgery, I had a septic infection. I remained in hospital for a week, then I was banned from swimming for six weeks. I needed to come up with a plan to be ready for Beijing without getting in the water. So we got an exercise bike at home, and every day I would cycle in the garage for hours; my mam still uses that exercise bike every day.

To be honest, I kind of struggle to explain where this level of dedication at such a young age comes from, because it's just so natural to me. It feels like trying to explain to somebody how to breathe. I think it's in every sportsperson, but I also think it's in every person. I think everyone's fully capable of it; it might just be a muscle they haven't flexed before. It's like riding a bike – you don't know how to ride a bike until you learn how to ride a bike. Once you know how, it's natural, and you do it almost without thinking.

Having something in your life that means so much to you that you can give it that much focus and dedication is something I joke about with other swimmers. We ask each other, 'Are we addicted to it? Is it a healthy addiction?! Are we a little bit insane?!' It does feel a bit like an addiction. I guess that's kind of why I'm so vocal about my retirement, because I don't want to go to Paris, have an amazing time, and then be like, 'Oh my God, I'm going to stay another four years!' I know that is quite likely to happen, because it happens after every Games. You get hooked, so sucked into the lifestyle, and addicted to the routine and the way of life, and you don't know how to stop. It's been a great life. But I'm glad that I can recognise that I want to try other things.

Even as a kid, I had tunnel vision about my goal. I just didn't see anything else; nothing else mattered. It was like I had been told, 'Do this, and you'll get to go to Disneyland, or meet Santa.' Beijing held that much appeal. So even though it was a goal I hadn't really set for myself, it did have an emotional attachment.

After Beijing, I struggled to juggle being a teenager with being an athlete. I was in an adult world from such a young age, but I wasn't an adult, so I didn't properly understand what it took to achieve the goals of that world. I didn't understand the consequences of my actions, and why I wasn't allowed to do certain things. When it was suggested that I could not do the same things my friends were doing, I felt like I was being controlled, and in frustration, I would rebel. As a teenager, your emotions are heightened, and I made decisions out of this emotional place. I would choose to go out with my friends and then go training three hours later. Obviously, this impacted on how I performed in the pool, impeding my progress.

When I look back now at my teenage self, and the kind of discipline and dedication that was required of me, I guess I feel sad. Because I didn't understand what was required, and I wasn't really taught. That meant that it felt like I was constantly in a battle, not doing as well as was expected of me, but not knowing how to do better. I would have loved someone older than me to advise me, sort of like a big sibling who had done it before, or just someone in their twenties. If I could go back to my teenage self now I would say, 'Stop messing.' But at the time, I couldn't see the bigger picture. If I could have, I wouldn't have found it so difficult to make better decisions. But that is a lot for a young kid to understand. I think also because it often wasn't positive feedback I was getting, it was all very negative, you kind of want to rebel against that. I think if I had had a bit more positive feedback, or positive experiences, maybe that would have encouraged me to make better decisions.

All of this meant that when I went to the London Games, aged 17, I failed to achieve a medal, and I was devastated over how I had performed, feeling that this was a missed opportunity. I knew I was better than that. But at the same time, I had been chasing goals set by others; I hadn't *really* connected with them emotionally. I finished the Games feeling like I had not lived up to my potential.

It was this sense of failure that forced me to realise what was important, what *I* wanted to achieve. Not living up to my potential forced me to set goals myself for the first time. I needed to get clear about what exactly were the goals I really cared about, and then make a plan.

Listen to yourself

My coaches had always told me I was a really good medley swimmer, a really good butterflyer, but I always wanted to swim breaststroke. For so long I listened to other people. It meant I wasn't achieving my potential because I didn't connect with those goals – they were just things I was told I should do. I knew deep down that I wanted to achieve in breaststroke. Eventually, it was about trusting my gut and believing that I was capable of doing what I wanted to do, and really committing to it.

I needed to have the confidence to listen to my gut and let my inner voice be my compass.

Try it.

Is there something, even vaguely at the back of your head, that you want to do, but are not quite willing to acknowledge even to yourself? Try imagining yourself in that situation you aspire to. Talk to others who have achieved the thing you want. How do you feel when you do this? Are you forming an emotional attachment to this outcome?

After I retire from swimming, I really want to work in radio as a broadcaster, but everyone always tells me I should do TV. I would love to end up trying to do both, but I'm going to prioritise radio, because that's what I've always wanted to do. The thought of getting up at 4 a.m. for a radio station doesn't faze me ... I think I'd find it a little harder for TV.

Ask yourself how a potential goal makes you feel.

Excited? Hopeful? When you really want something, the hard things don't seem like an issue. You will always figure out a way of doing the things you love.

A goal requires hard work, but some part of it should also feel like pushing at an open door. You should naturally gravitate towards it.

What makes you feel like yourself, gives you a sense of coming home to a positive version of you? What makes you feel most at ease in your body? If it's something that makes you feel alive right now, that's worth pursuing.

For me, goals are usually achieved in four-year cycles, with the Games at the end. To begin with, I will ask myself, 'At the end of a cycle, what do I want to look like?' I will envision myself at the end of the timeline I have set for the goal. Who is that Ellen? How has she changed from how she is now?

When it comes to figuring out what my goals are, and really setting intentions, I need to sit down and think deeply about why I want to achieve something, what makes it important to me, and then write it down. I find writing it down empowering; it's like making a contract with myself.

First, before I consider my goal, I write down all of the things that I want to let go of from the past. By doing this, I get it out of my head. Then I can write down all the things I *want* to happen. That's how I get my goals. Find a method that works for you. Because I like to doodle, I love a blank notebook. The more blank, the fewer lines, the more freeing it is.

Sometimes when I'm visualising my stroke or body position, I'll start doodling it. I'm not artistic – it could be a sketched line that will mean something to me about a position in the pool. That doesn't matter; it's getting it out on paper.

Whenever I go away, I'll always have a notebook with me. On the day itself, when the big goal comes around, I'll have the whole day written out with all the little things that I need to do.

It takes the pressure off. I don't have to think about what is involved in those last moments before hopefully achieving my goal – I just write it down, take a picture of it, make it my screensaver. I know what I am supposed to be doing at any time of the day. The small things create the pathway to my goal.

Once you have identified a big goal, look at what needs to happen on the way to achieving it, the incremental steps. Set some medium goals. For me, these could be something like big annual competitions, World or European championships.

Big, medium, small goals

Now break it down even further. You've set big ... medium ... now it's time for small goals. Give yourself weekly or even daily targets. These smaller goals are actually your most important ones. Achieving them builds the confidence you will need when the bigger goals are at your front door, ready to be faced. They are the foundational structure; small daily goals set and met stop your big goal creeping up on you and finding you unprepared.

When I am figuring out a goal, it helps to ask myself, 'Who do I want to be? What does she look like?' Whether it's a personal goal, or a swimming goal, it's about envisioning what it will look like when you achieve it, believing it, feeling it.

To commit to a goal, you need to connect emotionally with it. This makes it easier to accept the sacrifices that will come with achieving your goal. Missing out on things, setting boundaries around sleep, or cutting back on socialising – these don't feel like negatives when you know you are doing them for yourself. You can ask yourself, 'Am I going to be proud of myself for making that decision, or am I going to be annoyed?'

Clear goals help you make better decisions in the moment which will propel you towards what you want.

They help you figure out who you really are, what kind of person you want to be, what kind of life you wish to lead.

In personal goals, I will ask myself, 'What would the best version of myself be doing?'

As a professional athlete, I will think, 'What would a champion do or what would a winner do?'

There will have to be some sacrifices in achieving your goals. After *Dancing with the Stars*, I was invited to absolutely everything. It was so much fun, but after a while I couldn't keep up the juggle of it all. I would end up stressing and rushing and half-doing things. It got to the point where I realised I wasn't even enjoying things anymore; what I was doing wasn't making me happy, I was just showing up. So I had to take a back seat. I didn't *want* to miss out on certain things, but I had to. For my own self-care, I had to put boundaries around when I could do things and when I couldn't.

Sometimes, when it comes to achieving your goals, asserting boundaries applies to *really* lovely things, like spending time with people I love. One of my goals, about which I'm very strict, is that I have to get at least eight hours of sleep a night. To meet my curfew, guests need to leave my house at 10 p.m., because I need to be in bed at half 10.

Before you start on the journey to achieving a goal, it is necessary to identify and establish the boundaries around what it requires, so that when you are in doubt about whether you are on the right path, you can go back to your boundaries as your checklist.

There are times when I haven't achieved my goals, and it has always been partly because I have not stuck to my boundaries.

If you're struggling to complete your goals, break them down into a list of steps. Look at the first step, not beyond, and once you've completed that, you can move onto the second step. It's kind of like me going back to making my schedule for the day. The thought of race day can be so overwhelming, but once you break it up, you're just like, 'Oh, I do this first, then this ...' and it's just a matter of ticking things off. If eating your breakfast is the next thing on the list, you just eat your breakfast, and that's all that matters in that moment. That's what you're supposed to be doing.

Breaking things up into little steps really helps things to not become overwhelming; you can just take it one step at a time. That works for smaller, daily goals as well. I can be so messy sometimes, but even if I just take out the bins, my house is that little bit less messy. And then it's a little bit less overwhelming. Or just put a wash on. Something as simple as that, you begin to feel like, 'Oh actually, I can do this. This is OK. I might not do everything in the one day, but that's OK.'

Accountability

I don't recommend announcing your goals to the world, but I think telling certain people you trust about things you might struggle with, so that they can hold you accountable, can be helpful.

I have coaches who hold me accountable, but also my boyfriend helps with this. He knows my goals, and what is involved in meeting them, and while he won't ever tell me what to do, he might just remind me, or bring up the question, 'Are you sure you want to do that?'

Nobody has to know everything, but if one person knows something, then you have that person holding you accountable for one of the little things that you want to achieve. It takes the pressure or burden off somewhat; it's so much easier to show up for someone else than it is for yourself.

Don't be rigid about things. Be flexible with your timeline; you might need to adjust the period of time you have initially set yourself to achieve your goal, make it bigger or smaller. There is always room for growth, and for change. Always have a growth mindset. Always be coachable, always be open to being taught. Never assume that you know everything when you walk into a room; always ask what you can learn from someone else. You don't know who could inspire you.

CHAPTER CHALLENGES

Small – Write down all the things you want to let go of, and then the things you would like to set as goals. Take your time with it, maybe go away and come back to it several times.

Medium – Once you have identified the big goals, consider what it will take to get to them. Break it down to medium and smaller goals.

Big – Check in with yourself. Is what you have set yourself achievable, are your goals making you feel good about yourself, is the timeline you have set realistic? Do you need to make any changes?

six

Communicate

Don't be afraid to ask questions. Don't be afraid to ask for help when you need it. I do that every day. Asking for help isn't a sign of weakness, it's a sign of strength.

Barack Obama

When I broke up with my ex-boyfriend a few years ago, and he was moving out, even though I was only beginning to get my head around what had happened and had barely yet spoken to even my family or closest friends, I had to immediately tell my coach. At the time, I didn't remotely feel like confiding – I actually felt like crawling into a hole and not talking to anyone – but I knew what was going on was going to affect how I was performing in the pool, and because of that he needed to know. I knew I was going to struggle for a while and he would wonder why I wasn't swimming faster. Once he knew what was happening, he would be able to support me, rather than being in the dark.

People can't help you unless you ask for help. No matter how much you might want to be alone, go to ground, and not talk to anyone when you're suffering, unless you open up and are prepared to be vulnerable, you will remain isolated, and it will probably make everything so much harder.

It hasn't been just break-ups that I have had to learn to communicate about. If I haven't had enough sleep, or I'm having a hard time at college or school, or even if I'm feeling worn out for some reason, I have come to realise that I have to be able to communicate with my coaches and the staff I work with about how I'm feeling, let them in on whatever is going on. If I'm going through a hard time, I know I won't be able for a really heavy training session because my energy is going to be wiped. But I really didn't find communication like this easy to begin with.

Learning how to communicate made my life easier, but I had to learn it the hard way.

Between Beijing and London as a teenager, I didn't really understand what was going on, why I wasn't improving the way I wanted to and my coaches thought I should be, so I struggled to tell people how I was feeling.

Feeling insecure and alone, and constantly trying to hide my arm, was taking up a lot of energy. There was a real emotional drain in holding it all in, carrying the weight of all that worry and fear and stress. There was nobody for me to talk to who I felt would be able to help me. Sometimes, as well, you worry that it just sounds like excuses.

Learning to trust

I have learned since then that if you are communicating with someone with whom you have a good relationship, it will not sound like excuses, because there is a basis of trust there.

As I've gotten older, become an adult, my relationship with my coach has gotten so much better, and we've really learned how to communicate with each other. I now feel comfortable enough to tell him when I am sick or when I am struggling. Because there is trust between us, and he knows the kind of person I am, I feel safe to communicate honestly. He knows I'm not taking the piss.

I think if you have a track record that speaks for itself, and because of that people respect you, then whenever you do need to say something, they will believe you. And to be honest, even if others don't believe you or necessarily agree with you, if you have that trust in yourself, you will learn to be able to communicate honestly, put yourself first and do what's right for you.

If people are unhappy about it, they're unhappy about it; so be it. You know the boundaries you have to set for yourself, and when you have a strong sense of them, because you know what you need and you know that you come first, then straightforward, honest communication is so much easier. It can almost become hard *not* to communicate honestly and openly. Nothing is as important as your own happiness, and your own mental health.

Because of this invisible emotional drain when I wasn't communicating, I was always sick, and my energy was often low, because I was battling with my own internal demons, but then also having to train hard. At times, the people I was working with got angry because it just seemed like I wasn't looking after myself, or not taking my training seriously in some way.

I didn't know how to explain it to the people I was working with. I was eating relatively well, mostly sleeping well. Conversations about mental health were only starting to become a thing when I was a teenager, it wasn't something people commonly spoke about or really understood, so it would have felt silly to try to explain how I was feeling. I don't think I could have even found the right words.

Whatever is going on, communication when you're a teenager can be hard. And I think because I felt so different, I didn't think that whatever I was feeling was valid. I didn't believe that anyone else could understand how I was feeling.

At boarding school in England when I was fifteen, I went to a counsellor. I was in such a hole that I finally felt like it was time to talk to someone. I was in a really bad relationship, and just generally homesick on top of it, and I needed to talk about what was going on. Afterwards I felt so much better.

But then, unfortunately, the counsellor told my housemaster that I had been to see them. I was called in, and essentially belittled, told that my problems were all just kids' stuff, nothing that would matter in five years' time. That everything I was feeling would all mean nothing in the grand scheme of things. I never went back to that counsellor, because I didn't feel like it was safe. The trust essential for honest communication was gone, which was really upsetting, as I had really felt the benefit of going, and had felt so light afterwards, as if I had unburdened myself of some of the emotional weight I was carrying. I have learned since that trust, and a sense of safety, are crucial when you're opening up about important stuff.

The right person

I have had subsequent experiences with psychologists that have been more helpful. It's important to say that you need to find the right person for *you*. Because I have worked with sports psychologists, or psychologists in general, who were not who I needed, and we didn't get on, or we clashed, or I didn't trust them. You need to be so comfortable with the person that you're having these conversations with.

It isn't necessarily anything to do with the other person, or how professional they are. Sometimes you simply don't match. So I have hopped around psychologists over the years, trying everyone out, to see who's the right fit. Cinderella with the shoe! There's nothing wrong with this. Finding a person you can open up to isn't necessarily straightforward, but it's so important to spend time getting it right, rather than settling for someone you're not 100% comfortable with, because you ultimately will not feel comfortable communicating with them.

Even when it is good, that doesn't mean it won't be hard, especially at the start. You might feel like you don't know what to say, how to start the conversation, or what you need out of these interactions. It's normal to question what you're feeling, maybe even worry that you're being over the top, exaggerating. It's unlikely that you are.

Just dive in. When I work with psychologists, I'll sometimes literally just blurt things out. It can feel super awkward at the time, but it gets things moving. Sometime when I message my psychologist for an appointment, they might not be able to see me for a while, so I will write down why I needed to see them, a reminder for myself, because there's been so many times when I might be spiralling, in a really bad place, but then by the time I see them I'm fine. And we just stare at each other, with nothing to say. So I have found it handy to remember what I originally needed to talk to them about.

I think for a long time, I wasn't able to confront my feelings because I was afraid. Afraid of how big my emotions might be. And afraid of acknowledging them. As if, if I just continued to ignore them, somehow they would eventually go away. Which of course was never going to happen!

In fact, I now feel that *sometimes I have to hurt to heal.* I realise I won't feel better until I move through the big, uncomfortable emotions. Sometimes, I mightn't yet be ready, or strong enough for that hurt, so I will avoid it until I feel strong enough to feel that pain. But the important thing is that you do feel that pain eventually. Because you have to. Otherwise, by trying to ignore it, in fact you're just hanging onto it.

Speaking out

I spent years doing this, hiding, denying, running from how I felt. Then one day, before the Rio Games, when I was 20, I did an interview for *Winning Streak*. The person interviewing me asked, 'Have you ever been insecure about your arm?'

And I just honestly answered the question – the first time I had ever done so.

I had never been asked that question before. That was the first time that anyone had ever acknowledged that it might be a thing. And that was the first time that I ever was like, 'Oh, yeah, OK, of course.'

I think that's one of the big reasons I struggled for so long, because no one *had* ever asked me that. So I didn't know it was normal to feel the way I did. In some way their question kind of gave permission to how I had been silently feeling for years. I feel like I got stronger and braver, and more confident, because somebody *finally* asked me that question; it was a kind of acknowledgment. I don't think I even realised I needed to be asked that question. But as soon as I gave my answer, and I saw the feedback that immediately came flooding in, people saying they felt the same, I truly realised how important it is to talk about this. And I began to find it bizarre that no one had talked about it before. I think that's why I was so insecure, and that's why I had so many complicated feelings about my arm, because no one was acknowledging it!

What I had said in the interview was, 'I've just had to learn to do things a different way … with my arm I'd never really had a problem with it, but as I became older, and became a teenager, everyone has their insecurities, mine just became my arm. But with swimming, I couldn't really hide, all I had was my swimsuit, my hat and my goggles, so swimming gave me the confidence to just be who I was.'

I had never gotten such feedback from an interview before.

It made me realise the power in being vulnerable, and in communicating honestly about how I was feeling.

For me, saying it aloud meant it felt as if my insecurities no longer had such a hold over me anymore. I named the thing no one else was talking about, and that felt powerful. I saw that there was a need to talk about things, and a power in sharing it. Not just power, but connection.

Speaking out made me realise that I wasn't special, in a really good way. Anything that any of us in the world go through, we're not special – no one of us is the only one to go through an experience. There will always be someone who understands, if you just speak up.

It was so comforting to realise that I wasn't alone in this. That there are other people who've been through something similar, or who are still going through it. Talking about it helped so much. Even now, my friends and I will still talk about things that bother us sometimes. It might just be something that is frustrating us; *people are really staring today, aren't they? That's annoying.* Talking about it always helps us.

Creating connections

Communicating didn't just make me feel better in the moment, it made me closer to people as well. If a friend opens up to you about something, your immediate reaction is to be there for them, or to do whatever you need to do to help them. Sharing vulnerable moments creates intimacy within relationships. Without good communication, it's nearly as if you are not doing your friendships justice. If you don't open up, you don't give people the opportunity to help you, and to be close to you. You're potentially stifling connection with the people around you.

Showing a vulnerable side of yourself, even when you do it with strangers, humanises you. You will find a connection with someone. Even if they don't understand the specific thought process or experience that you have been through, they are still going to understand the feeling.

We all know what it is like to feel certain things.

The London Paralympics, in 2012, were something of a turning point for people with disabilities in the UK. There was so much advertising of different bodies all over the country, it really showcased what they could do, and went some way towards helping to change people's perceptions of disability, simply because they were exposed to disabled people more than usual. A friend of mine was put on a poster that took up the whole side of a building. It was an incredibly powerful image that made her unforgettable. Then several months later I was giving a talk at the company of one of my sponsors, Citi, and I mentioned this poster and how incredible it was to see someone with a disability being made so visible. Do you know that phrase, 'If you don't ask for something, you won't get it'? I was joking about how incredible it would be to see more disabled bodies on the sides of buildings. A few months later, they had put me on a poster on the side of their building in Dublin.

I think you will often find, once you do speak up, that people are generally really willing to make a difference; you just need to be brave enough to communicate, so they can hear about your experience, know what it is like to be you, and know what is needed.

That interview made me feel seen in a way that I hadn't ever before. And it made me realise, 'If I'm feeling like that, and if talking about it is helping me feel better, then it's doing the same thing for other people as well.' That's really what pushes me – it's so powerful when things like that happen, when you know what you are saying is meaningful to others.

As I got older, I knew I needed to figure out a new way of communicating within work. When you grow up within an industry, it can be hard to make the transition from child to adult in terms of how those around you treat you, and how they listen to you.

The people I worked with every day had known me since I was twelve, they had had to mind me as a kid, and as I got older I began to feel like they still saw me as a child, even though I was now in my twenties. It felt like my opinion was sometimes considered invalid, because I was still considered to be a child.

Finding my way to communicating like an adult, in a manner that made me feel like I was being taken seriously, wasn't straightforward. Initially, I worked with my sports psychologist, then had meetings with the staff. I had to learn to be direct. As I learned how to communicate as an adult, I have been trusted more, and left to do my own thing.

Straight talking

Now I can vocalise any issues in a very straightforward way with my coach, even about slightly awkward matters, like when I forget to input the information into our daily monitoring programme and miss the deadline. Before, I would have avoided letting my coach know, but now I will just send a message. *Sorry, I didn't do it.*

I improved at communication through a kind of exposure therapy; doing the thing you're afraid of doing, again and again. I've tried to do a lot of that; I first learned how to do it from going into college with my sleeve rolled up. I was terrified, but I pushed myself, and eventually, it became easier. Now, I've seen it play out, what can happen when you try something you're afraid of doing. I've seen how empowering the results are.

None of this is to suggest I communicate with ease at all times now. On occasion, I still notice myself going quiet, and it's always because I am in a situation where I feel like I don't belong. On these occasions, I might challenge myself to make conversation, and to try and get to know the people I'm with, try to find common ground. But if that doesn't work, I will stop, and just remove myself from the situation. Because unless it's something really, really important, where I *have* to figure out how to belong in that setting and find a way of being my true, authentic self in that environment, then I will think to myself, *this actually doesn't matter. Why am I wasting my energy on this?*

So now, it's not just about being *able* to communicate, but knowing *when* to. I have boundaries with myself, and I know when I'm not doing myself any good, when I'm not respecting myself by wasting my energy. I have come to recognise that my time is as precious as anyone else's. Sometimes what is needed, rather than communicating, is simply removing yourself from a situation.

It is somewhat ironic that I have gone from being someone who often found it hard to speak up in a room full of her peers to wanting to go into a career in communications when I retire from swimming. But during some of the times when I was at my most isolated, I found listening to the radio hugely comforting. When I was away on my own, or at times when I struggled to make friends or communicate with the people around me, I always had a friend in the radio. It was familiar, I didn't have to do anything, the presenters' voices became my friends. I think that is one of the reasons I want to pursue radio as a career – because it has been so comforting to me. The power of it, the ability to make someone who's alone feel connected.

TV is different. In that, I feel a responsibility to be visual for other people. For other people to see a disabled person being stylish, or wearing makeup, or just being happy. I think that's such a powerful thing, just seeing a disabled person happy, and it being more about their presence rather than their body. TV can communicate that in a way radio can't. It's a narrative we don't often see, a disabled person simply being themselves. TV appearances allow me to create my own narrative rather than just accept the ones that are placed upon me.

Sometimes, I can feel the weight of it. I can get burnt out by advocating. I think when it comes to seeing people with disabilities in the media, it's kind of like exposure therapy for society, in a way. It's like tricking people's brains into realising, *that's just a person*. The more exposure there is to people with disabilities, the more they realise, *that's just that person. They love fashion.* Or whatever it is that that particular person is into.

I try not to overthink it – I think that's important as well, because when you overthink it, you're feeding into the narrative of the whole weight of the disability. So just me being me when I'm on TV is probably the most powerful thing I can do. Or just me being me when I get dressed up and go out, and not hiding myself.

When a group of people with disabilities come together, because we don't see each other's disabilities, we are more able to recognise the obstacles in each other's way. I might meet a person in a wheelchair, who I've never met before, and without thinking walk up the ramp with them. Or hold the door automatically for them. It's just an automatic thing now, because I've been so exposed to people with disabilities. I don't look at them and go, *oh, they're in a wheelchair*, it's more that I look at the world around us, and think, *there's steps over there so we're clearly not going to go that way.*

Ableism is a word that a lot of people don't even know. And that in itself is nearly a form of ableism. Because by not even knowing the term, they're not even acknowledging that there is a problem. As humans, we're getting so much better at calling out racism and homophobia, and inequality in marginalised groups (although there's still a long way to go on all fronts), but for some reason disability is often forgotten.

It's almost as if some people think we don't have the same feelings and emotions as other human beings – but we do.

CHAPTER CHALLENGES

Small – Despite the fact that you may really not feel like reaching out, make a plan with a good friend, and stick to it. It can be something small, even just a phone call, but make a plan with someone who you trust, and have an honest conversation with them about how you are feeling. Note down how you feel afterwards. Lighter? Reassured? Less alone?

Medium – Consider your boundaries. Are you wasting time and energy trying to connect with people with whom you just do not click? Is it time to take yourself out of these situations, and instead protect your energy? Think of the people in your life with whom you spend the most time, and how you feel around each of them. Drained, or uplifted? Safe, or fizzy and anxious? Rethink who you share your vulnerable, honest moments with if necessary. Make a list of the people with whom communicating honestly feels comfortable, not scary, and focus on time with them.

Big – Practise direct communication. Consider a situation in your life that is simply not working for you, and in simple, short sentences, tell the person involved how you feel. Work out the points you want to make in advance, ideally not too many, and stick to those throughout. This may feel excruciatingly uncomfortable to begin with. It will get easier, and eventually you will feel much lighter after communicating openly, and so proud of yourself. The self-respect you gain in these moments will spur you on to further open communications, and attract people who are of a similar mindset: direct, honest, open. People who welcome your honesty because they value your friendship.

Dear 20-year-old me,

If only you could see how close you are. If only you could see that the only thing holding you back right now is your ability to believe in yourself. Your ability to be kind to yourself. You think you have conquered all your fears because you learned to love your arm. But it's more complicated. You've spent years putting yourself down, doubting your self-worth. You need to reprogramme your mind. You need to learn to train your thoughts like your body. It'll take some time, but you'll get there. I promise.

I wish you could also see how beautiful you are. It's funny. I look at pictures of you now, and I think, wow, how pretty I was, but I know you don't believe that. In eight years, you won't be able to see the flaws you do today.

I'm really proud of how independent you are. I know your attitude is that you need to do this on your own. And yes, you have to take on a certain amount of responsibility and ownership. But you are not alone. I wish you were capable of asking for help when you need it. I hope you realise that your parents will always be your parents whether you live at home or not. Lean into them more; they only want what's best for you.

Communication is key. No one can help you if they don't know what's happening. Start communicating better in college and in the pool. Nobody wants you to fail. When you succeed, everyone around you succeeds. Swimming may be an individual sport, but that doesn't mean you're alone. Teamwork will help you achieve your dreams. You are not an expert at everything. Use the people around you because that's what they are there for.

You're on the path to becoming so happy and so confident, so thank you for that. Your future is so bright and so exciting. Just keep doing the little things right, and you'll start believing in yourself.

It's OK not to have all the answers right now. Stop being so hard on yourself.

Love you lots,
28-year-old you x

seven

Laugh

Laugh often, laugh loudly, and most important, laugh at yourself.

Chelsea Handler

Laughter has always been the best way I have to show people that I'm a human being. That actually I'm just the same as everyone else. Disability can be so heavy, and something that people just don't understand. It's definitely different now, but in my school years, disability wasn't something people were taught about. There was little awareness, and very limited visibility of people who were disabled. This can be very othering, and can also mean the focus is on the negative, on what disabled people cannot do. What are the limitations?

Laughter gets beyond these tired, unhelpful, long-established narratives that it feels like people with disabilities sometimes are just expected to receive about themselves. It's because there is so much power in it, to connect, to defuse a situation, to shift the focus, lighten things up.

If I'm doing a talk, I always know that once I can make the audience laugh, they will relax and feel like they can relate to me a bit. We have found common ground, made a small connection which I can then build upon. Making people laugh, finding something that we all find funny, makes everyone feel safe. Making people laugh, *with* you, obviously, not *at* you, takes away the fear that can exist around disability, especially with kids.

That can sometimes be the hardest part about being different and being disabled – the fact that some people are going to be afraid of you. It's especially hard when a kid is afraid of you; there's so little you can do in those moments to change how they are reacting to you. As much as you might say. 'Look, it's safe, it's OK, I'm fine,' you can't force that on a kid who is terrified of you. Which happens. You kind of have to accept that they're afraid of you, which is really hard. But sometimes, even then, laughter can take the sting out of these moments.

Lighten up

If I'm making people laugh with me, and I'm showing the perks and the benefits of being disabled, and lifting the mood on it, making them see that I am a person who is funny and happy, I'm dissipating that fear and breaking down their stereotyped beliefs about me. I also feel that it's giving someone else with a disability an opportunity to not be judged as well; if they can see me do it, they might try it too, and see the benefits of laughter. Anything I can do to help others who have felt the weight of being different makes me really happy.

I have a story in my head about how people's perceptions of disability go. I don't feel I made it up; if I think it, it's likely the majority of people my age will think it, or even the majority of people in Ireland. The story is that disability is always cast as, *oh, that poor person*. Or the focus is always on the things a person with a disability cannot do. And when they do something unexpected, it's, *oh my God, aren't they incredible? A triumph, an outlier.* I like to try to provide a counter-narrative. To show that I'm just trying to live my life like everyone else. I'm neither a victim nor a hero. *Oh and hey, look, these are the perks I have because I am a disabled woman: half price nails, and I get to skip the queue in Disneyland!* Like I said, laughter lightens things.

For me, creating this dynamic makes me feel like a person when people's reactions to my disability have made me feel excluded. It means that the attention isn't on my arm; when they're laughing, they're laughing with me, my arm isn't an issue, and I'm taking control of the narrative, rather than passively receiving the reactions of others, the stares and awkward questions or incorrect assumptions about my abilities.

It's always so important to me to not be the reason someone feels a negative emotion; I don't want to be the reason anyone is uncomfortable or scared or sad. I guess it's just because I grew up feeling so uncomfortable my whole life. I was rarely happy in my own skin. It probably is something I have to work on myself,

LAUGH

because it's probably restricting me from being the complete version of me, because I'm still, in a way, trying to people-please. But I would rather just be the reason that someone feels a little bit better than be the reason they feel a little bit worse.

Own your narrative

As I have written already, when I was a teenager, being different was the worst thing in the world. But once I started to embrace it, I slowly came to realise it's the best thing ever. I began to love being different. My younger self could never have imagined that I would feel the way I do now, but *I love that people will always remember me. That my arm makes me completely unique.*

When I was a kid in primary school, even though I hadn't been othered, or picked on or anything like that, I was still aware that I had one arm and I always wanted to have two hands, even though I wasn't really insecure about it or anything. I just always wanted to be like everyone else. But as an adult, if you gave me the option, I wouldn't want it. Now I am happy to stand out, I have become *entirely* comfortable in my own skin.

That's been my whole life, people staring at me, and it can be quite heavy. But ... if people are going to stare at me, what do I want them to see when they do?

It is this kind of thinking that inspired me to get the tattoo on my arm, a koi fish and cherry blossoms; it's for Japan and Tokyo. I have always thought, *wouldn't it be class to have a tattoo sleeve on my arm, to make people look at my arm rather than trying to hide it?* Look at me and see what it is like. It's not scary, and I will no longer hide pieces of myself away, feel any shame. Instead, I like to adorn my arm, make it pretty. I rarely wear a prosthetic, but at an event recently, I wore a bejewelled prosthetic; I get to accessorise my arm. It's what makes me stand out. People are going to look anyway, so now I try to embrace that. To own it.

It was my idea to create the bejewelled prosthetic; it was just something fun that I thought I could do. I had been putting it off for so long, and I just got to the point where I was like, *fuck it, I need to do this.* It took so long to create! I'm still finding diamantés all over my house. I still have the arm in my sitting room, on the coffee table as a piece of art now. It's my accessory that I can wear at any point.

I lean into my arm as my superpower so much because I felt so negatively about it for so long, but now, as an adult, so many of the things that I do, and the opportunities that I get, are all because I have one arm, and because I'm different. My arm *gets* me places, and now, it gives me my confidence. It's always a talking point, and it's kind of weirdly comforting knowing that I'm not going to be easy to forget.

I love sport movies generally, but there's a scene from one in particular, *Coach Carter*, that has really meant a lot to me, when one of the athletes, quoting Marianne Williamson, tells the basketball team, 'Our deepest fear is not that we are inadequate. Our deepest fear is that we are powerful beyond measure. It is our light, not our darkness, that most frightens us. Your playing small does not serve the world.'

When you refuse to diminish yourself, you give other people permission, or even courage, to do the same. Initially, for me, it wasn't about anyone else. When I started rolling up my sleeve at the beginning of college, that was for me alone, that was personal. It was a battle I was having in my head; no one else knew what I was doing, only me, and I didn't think about how my actions might impact others.

I didn't quite expect the impact it would have on me.

When I started talking about my arm in interviews and allowing people to hear my story, and saw how they related to it, I came to realise that no matter how different you are, you're never alone. There will always be others who have experienced something of what you have, and who will understand. As soon as I started talking about it, I'd get so many people getting in touch to say, 'I never knew that; I'm exactly the same.' Messages from parents of kids saying their child had been hiding her arm and now she wasn't, after seeing my interview. That's incredibly powerful. It makes me feel like I am part of a community and that I'm not alone. We might not have identical experiences, but we understand how it feels to be different.

Unforgettable

When I'm talking to kids, I always tell the story of meeting Danny, the lead singer from The Coronas, at an awards ceremony after the Rio Games. We were chatting when he gave me his email address, and said, 'Get in contact, I'll get you tickets for the next gig, just send me a message.' When I was sending him the email, I wrote, 'Hi, this is Ellen, the girl with one arm. I hope you remember me.' He got back saying, 'Of course I remember you.'

I am a disabled woman. And there's a lot of people who don't even identify as disabled. But for me, it's important to identify as disabled, because that means I'm taking ownership of it. And finding the pride in it, because in my experience, the things we're insecure about become bigger if we don't take ownership of them.

No one's ever going to forget me; it is my superpower, my arm. It is the thing that makes me different, uniquely me. That's class, that's *magical*. As long as you take control of it and don't let it control you. Own it.

CHAPTER CHALLENGES

Small – Consider the thing that makes you wonderfully unique, unforgettable. Even if at first you're not sure how you feel about that thing, whatever it is, try leaning into it, the uniqueness of you.

Medium – Watch one of your favourite movies that you know will make you laugh. Even better, get a group of friends around to do it with you. Lose yourself in the moment. Embrace escaping, tuning out. Forget for a couple of hours whatever it is you are dealing with.

Big – Keep things light. Organise a night out with friends to a comedy show. If things are feeling heavy, rather than trying to wrestle with them, turn away from them towards something, or someone, that will make you laugh. We cannot always solve what we are dealing with in the moment, when we are weighed down by the heaviness of a situation. Find an activity you know will make you laugh. Taking a moment of levity will not just make you feel better, it might just open things out to create solutions and new pathways you hadn't even realised were there.

eight

Cry

I don't think
sadness is always
devastating. It can be
quite uplifting and
joyful as well and
sometimes, you have
to let yourself be
sad in order to move
forward.

Adele

I have one specific friend who I will call whenever I need a cry. It goes both ways; we do it to each other. We both understand that it is a matter of having a safe person you can let go in front of.

I like having someone there when I cry over sad things; it's a way of not feeling alone through it, and of having the safety of someone else being there. Sometimes I'll realise I haven't cried in a while, and think, *I really should just find someone to cry to!* I will know when I need a good cry: there is a heaviness and maybe a sluggishness in my body. I will realise that it feels as if I'm carrying a bit of a load, and that I might have been feeling this way for a while, but just not really noticed, or ignored it. I might not be looking after myself well enough. That's when I know I need to cry.

CRY

I think crying can help when there are emotions that are too big yet for you to process, or feelings you don't quite fully understand yet, but you need to get them out. The only way to do it is to release them. That's what crying does for me. When I can't think it through, or talk it through, I'll cry it out.

Learn to let it out

I always feel such a release when I cry. I could be feeling shit for days and not know what's wrong, and then if I have a big cry, I just instantly feel so much better, as if I've shed a layer and now I'm renewed. It's so important to let all those big emotions out.

Having someone there also means you get to enjoy the giddy laughter that comes after the release of a big cry. The person you cry in front of needs to be the right person. Someone who will just let you at it, and not make such a fuss over what's happening that you end up having to reassure them. You need someone who isn't afraid at the sight of it. Who can accept the crying rather than worry about it and make you feel awkward. Allow you to feel safe in the moment, rather than concerned that you are worrying them. It's a lot! Sometimes, I would use therapy for this: to have someone there who it feels safe to cry with, but whose reaction I do not need to worry about.

At the time of writing, the last time I cried was probably at the 2023 World Championships last summer, after my race, knowing it was the beginning of the end of my swimming career. That's sad. But I know it just means I've been so lucky. And the crying helped me process that sadness.

Sadness can be scary, and I don't like feeling it, obviously, but it's a really strong emotion, and feeling it just means you're human.

I try to think that having something to be sad about means you had something that you cared about.

On autopilot

I tend to cry a lot on the plane home after an event. It's the emotion that this thing I have worked so long and hard for is officially over; I think of this as a kind of gratitude crying. I'm grateful for the experience, so there's a lot of emotion. It was the same with *Dancing with the Stars* – I would have cried when that was over, or when certain dances that meant a lot to me were over. I would have cried on my own with Stephen – although he cried a lot more than I did!

When I don't cry and I hold on to things, I risk going on autopilot. I'm not present and I can be avoidant: avoiding situations, or being present, because I am trying to avoid my feelings. Sometimes I think I need to nearly schedule in a cry, just to make sure there's nothing I'm unknowingly holding onto.

If you're struggling to cry but you do have that weighty feeling, I think music can really help. Put headphones on, lie down, listen to lyrics. Taylor Swift is a good one; she'll always work. Or Adele. Just get lost in the lyrics of things. Or watch a sad movie.

If you feel unsafe crying in front of someone, do it alone. Crying in front of someone can be the next step. There are people I would never cry in front of. You need to find someone who you feel will accept it, without overthinking it. Someone who will not judge you, with whom you feel comfortable expressing yourself.

Never feel like you have to share all of yourself with everyone. Sometimes people aren't capable of taking on another person's emotions because they already have so much of their own stuff they are processing. And that's OK. It doesn't mean they love you any less, they just don't have the capability to be what you need right now. In the same way, there may be some people who you are not able to be there for. It's about recognising that you can't today, which is hard, but it's a necessary boundary. Sometimes it's too heavy, and the impact will be too much, to let other people's stuff in. Communicating *why* you can't help is important and will help the other person still feel seen.

But when you do get the chance to cry, enjoy the release of it. You might just feel amazing.

So there's the kind of crying that happens with a friend, release crying, then there's the post-event happiness/gratitude crying, and then there is crying in the pool. For me, I think crying when I'm swimming is probably the loneliest crying. Because I have my goggles on, no one can see me. Whenever I've cried while swimming, it's either because I haven't done well, or I'm struggling with something. The pool can feel like the only place where I have complete privacy. I'm sealed off, and it's somewhere I can let go if I don't want anyone to see me cry. In those cases, I don't want comfort. I just need ... it's not even the release, I need to feel the pain of it.

Sometimes there are feelings you cannot process through talking. Certain things are just so private that even you yourself might not fully understand them yet, so you need to feel them. It's like I said at the outset of this book – sometimes talking might not be what you need. And it's not like when you need an emotional release around life just feeling a bit weighty, or things being overwhelming. Sometimes I find there are some things that hurt, and I need to feel the pain, because it helps me understand what has hurt me.

Processing in the pool

Swimming is like a form of meditation for me. It takes me away from everything else and focuses me on what I am doing in that moment. I'm very much in my own thoughts. This closed-off space can serve to bring up things I might not have consciously realised were there.

It can also help me process other difficult emotions, like anger. I do get angry, but it's a weird one. Rather than getting angry with other people, I am more likely to get angry with myself. Like, obviously other people piss me off, and I get frustrated by them, but anger is more something I direct at myself, for *allowing* myself to be upset at how other people's actions have made me feel. When I feel like this, the emotion is completely internalised.

In these instances, I need to be on my own. Because otherwise I'm just not a nice person; I snap, I have no patience. Obviously it's not pleasant being in the company of somebody like that, so I like to remove myself! I don't like anger controlling me. I just prefer to be on my own until it has passed, and I have figured out what is causing it.

Training can help with anger. Sometimes when I'm in the pool, I'll allow myself to get angry, because I can try and process the anger. And then I just have really good sessions! I turn the negativity into extra gains.

I think it's important to vocalise anger and get it out, but because I'm someone who is so bad at confrontation, it will take a lot for me to confront someone over something. I'll only really do it if it's a frequent thing. If someone just does something that annoys me once, I'll feel, *oh, that person is so annoying*, but I'll move on.

Being alone in the pool also gives me the space to really consider how I'm feeling before I react to something. I like to *really* reflect on things. If I'm upset with someone, I don't like reacting straight away, because I need to figure out what that emotion is first. I don't like giving people the wrong emotion. I need some time, to know exactly what it is that's nagging me or upsetting me, before I confront someone about something. Because when I do speak to them, I don't want the emotions to still be there, and then for them to be annoyed in response. I really like to understand my emotions, so when I reflect, I might even write down what I'm feeling. Being by myself when I'm swimming, I'm alone with my thoughts, just going up and down, which gives me the space to really think things through.

I think when it comes to processing big, difficult emotions, sadness, anger, it's a mixture of taking some time to yourself to let things settle and figure out what's really going on, how you're feeling, what it is that has upset you, and also finding people with whom you can safely communicate, show your sadness. I carried the weight of things for years. Learning where and how to let go lightens a burden you might not even realise you are carrying.

CHAPTER CHALLENGES

Small – Find some quiet, calm spot, and ask yourself how you are feeling. Try a body scan, slowly making your way through each part of yourself; are you holding stress somewhere in your body that you have yet to acknowledge in your mind? Allow yourself some quiet moments and try not to shy away from any difficult emotions. Even if they feel overwhelming at first, they will pass.

Medium – Organise a movie night with a friend, watching the weepiest movie you can think of. If there's no one you feel comfortable doing this with, plan an evening in on your own. Record how you feel afterwards in your notebook. What came up for you? How did it feel to cry it all out? Mind yourself in the days that follow. Get lots of rest, and watch out for any revelations that come to you; note them down.

Big – If you know you are struggling with big feelings that you are finding hard to articulate, maybe it's time to consider counselling. Talk to your GP. Reach out. Even if it feels awkward to begin with, talking to a professional, the right one for you, is always a good idea. Mental health is as important as physical health, and sometimes we need to work at it in the same way we work at exercising. If you don't know where to start, break it down into manageable pieces. Make a five-step plan in your notebook. ·

nine

Rest

Let's begin by taking a
smallish nap or two ...

A.A. Milne,
Winnie-the-Pooh

When you're an athlete, you really need to learn how to rest. For years I thought I knew how to rest – after all, how hard could it be? I took naps; from a young age they had been built into my schedule. On swim trips since I was 11, my coach would try and persuade me to have naps in between swimming sessions, even though for a young kid and then a teenager, that didn't necessarily feel natural. Nevertheless, I built it into my schedule – training hard, napping, training hard, sleeping – and for over a decade, I thought that's all that rest was: part of the schedule. An item on the to-do list, a box to be checked.

It was only when the pandemic began, throwing *all* schedules into disarray, that I began to really understand what *proper* rest is: very far from something you ticked off your to-do list!

REST

Throughout secondary school, every weekday and every Saturday morning, I would get up at 4.15 in the morning, and swim from 5 to 7, then do the same again every weekday evening as well. The only time I had to myself was Saturday evening, and all day Sunday. On my day off, my brain would feel like it was going to explode, I was so in my head, without the outlet of swimming to burn off excess mental energy. To this day I still sometimes hate Sundays, because I feel like I *should* be doing something to relax, which ironically makes it trickier to actually relax. Doing nothing is hard for me.

At the same time as I was doing this intense training schedule, I was always sick as a teenager. I'd get really bad sinusitis, and my sport-induced asthma would flare up a lot. I didn't understand then, but all of this was in part because I was so bad at resting; I simply didn't know how to. And so I was never properly restoring myself.

Initially, when the pandemic stopped everything I found it completely weird. I didn't know how to handle not doing what I have always done. As an athlete, your life is incredibly organised and structured; in my case I had been doing the same things since I was a small child, my days filled with the same routines. Suddenly, I wasn't able to do them anymore. My whole identity felt completely confused; who was I if I wasn't Ellen the swimmer? I had no idea what to do with my time and I really struggled to take advantage of all the free time.

Learning how to switch off

Right now I have a month off between the World Championships and beginning to train for the Paris Paralympics. That break is so important because I need to rest, I need to rejuvenate, I need to recover. And a form of that is just allowing myself to do whatever I want to do. Eating whatever, and spending my time however I want, sometimes just doing nothing. I am resting myself from the pretty set routine that I usually have.

There are things that are part of your life, some good, some maybe less good, but still part of it, that you will need to rest from at times. For me, one is my heavy training schedule. Another is the topic of disability. That's quite heavy, and I need to remove myself from that conversation at times, just to give myself a rest because my brain is going to explode otherwise. I mean proper switch-off rest, not just the nap that is built into the training schedule.

Sometimes I can be really, really overwhelmed, and I can't focus and there's just too much going on in my brain. I'll say to my coach, 'I just need a day.' He'll give me that day off from training, because he knows I'll come back a better version of myself tomorrow. On that day I could simply need to be at home, to be alone. I just need to decompress. Something has been too much; I've pushed myself too far in some aspect of my life. It could be my body, it could be my brain. It could just be that I'm tired. But it's important to be able to do that, and to be able to *recognise* when you need to do that. I come back a better person the next day. If I don't take that rest, and I don't take that break, it will impact the next day's training, and then the week that follows. Now I am able to acknowledge that I need some rest, it makes me a better athlete.

But when the pandemic hit, and my training schedule came to a sudden halt, I certainly didn't know how to rest. Until then, I had always felt as if rest was lazy, and a bad thing. Saying you needed to slow down or stop was the wrong thing to do. Now I understand it's actually the right thing to do, and it's probably the braver and smarter thing to do, but I had to learn that.

Absolutely unable to deal with the empty days which would have previously been filled with training and meetings, when lockdown began, I went into a kind of overdrive. I attacked the house I was living in with three housemates at the time in a kind of cleaning frenzy that I think scared them all!

The others became properly concerned at my cleaning efforts; I spent three days on the bathroom alone, then became outraged when one of them dared to shave his beard in the sink I had cleaned! I even deep cleaned the chimney! Things *really* got out of hand.

Nowadays I really like cleaning and tidying my house. It helps me to be in the moment, it's a kind of flow activity for me, and I enjoy spending time on my own. But this cleaning wasn't like that. It was the opposite, in fact: a rather extreme attempt to distract myself from being in my head, from the sudden stop we were all being forced to undergo.

At the same time, I was trying to keep up my training, which was difficult; my flatmates wanted to exercise together as something to do to pass the time, but I needed to maintain the standards expected of a professional, high-performance athlete, except in the temporary gym I had created in my back garden. It's my job, and I couldn't afford to let my training slide, especially as I knew that Tokyo was coming up. And of course, I couldn't get in the pool. Struggling, I moved in with a retired athlete turned coach from another sport. As a coach, they were focused on getting an athlete to qualify for Tokyo, so they understood what a high-performance athlete needed to try to achieve.

Once I moved there I had nothing else to do bar my training, and I finally began to rest. To relax. Once I did it, I actually found it was quite nice! I started slowing down. One day it took me three hours to finish a gym session that should have taken an hour. But now I had that time. The rest I was already taking became deeper; I started to sleep really well, and getting into bed became my favourite time of the day.

Off the hamster wheel

I still tried to fill my time – that habit didn't die fast – but instead I filled my days with peaceful things. Yoga, meditation, books. I began to feel as if I could hear myself think again, something I hadn't felt for a long time. And it began to bring me back to my *why*. Deep down I had known I wasn't ready for the original date of the Tokyo Games in 2020, now postponed because of Covid. Underneath I had been panicking, trying to get everything done.

REST

I hadn't been able to be present because I was worrying so much about the future, always thinking ahead. The mental strain was exhausting. And I was never resting enough to restore myself.

In the lead-up to Tokyo, and before the pandemic, I had been on a hamster wheel, and I hadn't ever stopped. I could see now that I had never really rested, instead believing I could endlessly push myself. Not only did I not understand proper, switched-off rest, I didn't see that it was an essential part of progressing my goals. Lockdown was the longest time I had ever been out of the water since I was 10. That's a long, long time. I had been feeling the pressure, and I wasn't really enjoying what I was doing any longer. It was only after I had rested because of lockdown that I really began to appreciate and enjoy it again.

Now, I'm really looking forward to Paris because of my goal; of course I would love to win a gold medal again, but my goal really is to enjoy it. It's my last Games, and I just want to live in the moment, appreciate it all and take it all in. That means the good days, that means the bad days. That means all the horrible training that I know is in my future! I'm just looking forward to it. I think it's probably going to be my best season yet, because I know it's coming to an end. Learning how to properly rest and restore myself has got me to this point, where I can look forward to something and know I will be able to be in the moment.

Being forced by lockdown to stop, as so many of us were, brought me into the present. Jarringly so at first, but after a time I acclimatised. Now everything I was doing had a considered purpose, rather than being part of a frantic rush to an impending finish line.

Beyond just the fact that slowing down and being forced to stop gave me space to find my voice a bit more, it also made me get to know myself better, rediscover bits of myself I had forgotten about, always rushing about, training, trying to fit it all in. I returned to reading and to other things I liked doing which I had abandoned for some time. Stuff I did because I enjoyed it, rather than because I had to.

I got back to taking my time with cooking. I began to enjoy cleaning and organising my space. Activities that allow me to be in my head, a place I began to love to occupy. I couldn't see it as it was happening in the moment, but the space that rest was creating in my life, and my head, was allowing me to get comfortable with myself.

I started to feel like a different person, one who was full of gratitude. I understood myself far more now, and with that came the realisation that constantly pushing myself was not the way to achieve what I wanted, and it certainly was not what was best for me. I came to see that I am at my best when I know what I need to replenish myself, and prioritise it, putting boundaries around things like how much sleep I need. Eight hours, by the way!

Stopping to get started

Stopping and resting created time to take stock in a sense. I came to realise I need downtime, time just to myself. Time when I am not ticking boxes off a to-do list or a schedule.

Just today, my coach texted me to say I don't have to train this evening. I'm not going to tell anyone. I'm just going to sit in my house by myself and enjoy the quiet. Previously I swam every evening bar one, but my coach and I scheduled in a weekly break from training on Thursday evenings. It provides some much-needed space for decompression, to detach for a few hours from the go, go, go, allow myself to settle, and in doing so, see what might come up. That evening off, usually spent at home in my own company, helped me to realise if I was overdoing it and needed to take better care of myself (usually the answer was yes).

After lockdown, when I went back to swimming, my new-found ability to properly rest meant I was present for every stroke, every hour I was in the pool. I was able to be in the moment, rather than constantly racing ahead, mentally at least, into the future, to all the things I needed to do to get where I wanted to be and achieve my goals.

The pandemic taught me how to have boundaries around my energy, that I needed to protect myself from things that drained me, to create little pockets of rest throughout my days and weeks. I've tried regular massages, reflexology and holistic therapies. Arriving at training early to allow for some quiet moments. I want to get to the point where I can meditate – I don't think I'm there yet, but I meditate in my own way in the pool, or even poolside. I find morning traffic very stressful, so now I try really hard to leave early for training. If I have to be at the pool at half four, I'll leave at half three. I might get to the pool at four, and I'll just sit there.

For me, that is kind of meditating. I'm not actively meditating but I'll just chill. I might scroll, I might read, I might close my eyes for five minutes, but I feel so much better than I do if I'm late and then everything is a rush.

I've recognised the things that stress me out and make me overwhelmed or mean I start overthinking. Technology is a big one, so I have restrictions on my phone now. That way, I feel like I'm in control of myself. I noticed, as well as my phone, if I spent loads of time on PlayStation or my Game Boy, I'd feel like such a waster afterwards. Like I had just wasted three hours of my life. I hate the feeling of waste, of not growing, but standing still. I hate it so much. So when I put those restrictions on, I feel a sense of control. And I feel a bit more confident in what I'm doing. That I'm actually being present, and living.

It's about creating quiet moments in my day where I become unstuck, even for a few moments, from the grind, the constant doing, thinking ahead; that's a form of rest for me.

Previously, my brain could be fried and all I could think was *go, go, go, go, go, go, go*. It would never have occurred to me that what I needed to do was stop pushing, slow down. My physio once had to come to the gym with me, to talk to my trainer about what pain levels we needed to stop training at, knowing that I would never say 'Stop', but would instead push through. Now I know that what I actually need is to stop. And I am able to text my coach and say, 'I can't today.' This is not to suggest that I can do any of this without experiencing guilt. There is absolutely guilt. As a sportsperson, it can be hard to lay claim to rest. Our work isn't delineated by weekends, or days off, and there's always a sense of guilt, of worry you are being weak. *What is my competitor doing?* You don't have a certain number of days off. The hard decision isn't to keep going. The hard decision is to stop.

We are so bad at looking after ourselves.

I think it shows there's a level of self-worth that we're lacking. We don't want to seem like we're making a fuss over ourselves. I don't ever want people to judge me for that. For example, I remember I always wanted to journal, but I'd be too embarrassed, because I wouldn't want people to judge me for journalling. But it's what I need to do, it's what I want to do, so why did it matter what other people thought of it? I think there's always going to be an internal judgement that we're afraid of.

Mind yourself

We mind other people. We don't mind ourselves. Sometimes to mind myself, I need to go into the headspace of treating myself like a child or like someone I love, because it's so much easier to do it then. You know, Beyoncé has her Sasha Fierce alter ego and that's why she's able to do what she does. You nearly have to talk yourself into it, separate from yourself slightly – *I need to mind this person*. Just because this person is you, doesn't make them less worthy of being cared for.

The grind is glamorised. People always say to me, 'Oh my God, you exercise so much.' But to me, what is really impressive is someone who has so much control they can walk away and say, 'I'm going to go to bed now.' Be that person who has so much control over their own boundaries. I get a little thrill now from having my own boundaries – rather than giving into FOMO, like I did when I was younger, I'm now able to say no.

I like having the control.

I think to myself, 'Who do I look up to and who do I want to become and what's the best version of myself and what does she look like?' And she looks like she has eight hours' sleep and isn't influenced by other people.

The important people are always going to be there. And in terms of making compromises and being able to make different plans, if they're important to you, they'll recognise what matters to you. And if they want to see you and spend time with you, it's going to have to be within your boundaries.

I think probably the biggest struggle of being an athlete is just being strong enough to admit that it's too much today. It's better for me to rest than it is for me to turn up. Because otherwise it will just continue, the cycle. I needed the cycle to break.

CHAPTER CHALLENGES

Small – Place boundaries around your phone. Look at different parts of your day when you could cut back on how much you're scrolling. Bedtime? Maybe it's a case of getting a new alarm and leaving the phone outside the room or, at the very least, having a cutoff point at night beyond which you do not look at your phone. Make a note of how it feels when you begin to use it less. Investigate any reminders you can place on your phone that let you know when you have been on it more than 15 minutes.

Medium – Build small blocks of rest, where you do nothing, into your day. Staring out the window on the commute into work (as long as you're not the driver!). Sitting on your bed after a shower in the evening, staring off into space, letting your mind roam.

Big – Plan some proper switched-off time. A few days, even a week, when you take time off work, and schedules, and doing, and simply just be. Try writing down in your notebook what a few days of rest would look and feel like. What would you do if all pressures were off, and it was simply about doing what you felt like?

ten

The Universe

Sometimes you think
you're being put in a
hard situation but in
reality the universe
is preparing you
for something good.
Remember that. And
be ready for when it
comes.

R.M. Drake

I've always envied people with religion. In sport, it seems to me like believing in something that is greater than you can take the pressure off. A sense of certainty, that greater forces are at play, and there is a set path.

Growing up, I believed in something (I just didn't really know what), but I lost any religion I had the older I got. My mam is really religious – every Christmas Eve night we all go with her to Mass – but I just wasn't, and after everything that happened with the Church I had no religious faith. Through competing, I have come across people who are religious, and it sometimes feels as if they are able to perform well *because* they believe so much in something larger than themselves. I used to crave that sense of faith, a belief in something beyond myself.

After the Rio Paralympic Games in 2016, I was left feeling a little bit lost; I hadn't performed as well as I had hoped and was disappointed I had not reached my potential. I remember over-hearing an athlete who won gold thanking God for pushing them. It struck me for the first time that I needed to believe in something bigger than myself. I realised I needed to let go, and trust. Trust that things would be OK. That they were happening for a reason, that my life, while in the moment may seem as if things were going awry, was actually on the correct path.

There had been moments in my life when I had had a gut feeling about something, and I hadn't listened to it, then later thought I should have had more belief in what I was feeling. That when it came to making decisions, I needed to listen to that inner instinct.

There was the time I ignored my gut feeling after a bad break-up from a not-great, on-and-off relationship. When I was dumped just as I was getting on a plane – class, thanks – my friend sitting beside me put on Beyoncé for the entire flight, just repeatedly playing the song 'The Best I Never Had'.

A few months later, that guy and I were talking about getting back together. When I went to pick him up, that same song came on the radio as I pulled up.

See the signs

I knew in that moment, *this is a sign, this is not right for me*, but I chose not to listen to it, instead telling myself I was going to ignore it. I really shouldn't have – I probably would have had a better experience of my final year. But often it's only in hindsight that you look back and think, *oh, OK, I should have listened to myself.*

When we make decisions that do not align with our core values, or which are not really for our benefit, there's often a kind of off feeling inside. It's your gut telling you this is not for you. Learn to listen to it, and to trust your own instincts. You know what is best for you.

I think knowing what your values are can really help with this. When you know the things that are important to you, that you stand for, in a way it helps with almost instinctively gravitating towards what best suits you.

For me, personal growth is a big one. So is feeling strong. I think that is an internalised thing because of my assumption that when people see me, they automatically assume I'm weak, because I'm disabled. So even if they can't see what I can do, *I* know what I can do. I know when I retire, I'll still go to the gym, because it gives me the feeling of knowing that I am strong physically, and that also gives me strength mentally.

Being kind is an important value for me; when I was in primary school, the slogan was *Treat Others the Way You Would Like to be Treated.* That *really* stuck with me! Another value is to be the person that I needed when I was a kid.

What is it you are listening out for when it comes to gut feeling? It's a sense of knowing, a niggling instinct that won't disappear, until you land on what is really right for you, and then things will settle within you, and there will be no more internal questioning.

If you tune into it, it helps you relax, rather than stress about outcomes, or trying to force situations. It can take a while to figure out the right thing. You could *really* want something to happen, but still know deep down it's not for you. Once you accept that, you can relax, rather than fight and struggle. With *Dancing with the Stars*, everyone kept telling me I was going to win, but I knew I wouldn't. I just knew, and I accepted that from the start. When we didn't win, I wasn't upset because it wasn't about that for me; it was just about getting as far as we did.

Now that I have started listening more to that inner compass, it's like it provides a buffer from things which previously might have been disappointing.

Sometimes the reverse happens: what seems like the wrong thing for you turns out to be right, and you just have to go with it. Looking back, I can pick out times now when events took a turn which at the time seemed like things had gone awry, but I can see now it happened for a reason.

After school, I didn't get the grades required to get into the communications course in DCU I had hoped for. Instead I ended up doing a culinary course. At the time, it wasn't my first choice, but I can see now it was the best thing. I met friends I still have today, learned about nutrition, and also found myself in a situation that allowed for the amount of room sport needed in my life, something that might not have happened if I had been studying Communications – where I might have tried to go into media while still swimming, diluting both paths, consumed by college and swimming, not able to give either enough focus.

On another occasion, there was an interview for a big fitness-related TV show. My agent was excited about the opportunity, and it did seem like it should be a perfect fit for me, but I just knew the right vibe wasn't there for me. It wasn't aligned, the right energy wasn't there. Not getting it wasn't remotely disappointing, because I knew inside that it was not meant for me. I was buffered, because I trusted my instinct.

Even when a relationship ends, and it can feel at times as if it might have been a negative thing in your life, if you re-examine it, sometimes you might see that a thing was there for a reason, that it served a certain purpose. That maybe someone supported you through a specific thing, and while ultimately it wasn't the right fit, it did happen for a reason.

There is peace to be found in letting go and trusting.

It's also about not being afraid to ask why something is such a struggle. If you simply cannot seem to make a thing work, if it is never straightforward, question it. Maybe it's not really for you, whether it's a job, a relationship, or a goal you're striving for.

When you do ask, maybe the answer might be, 'Because what you're chasing is not fitting your purpose.' It's not for you.

Listen to your body

Sometimes I think your body gives you clues; it can be really good at picking up on things that are good for you and bad for you. Listen to it. During one relationship, I was always sick, sinus problems, constantly run down, but as soon as we broke up all that stopped, and I felt better. My body had been sending me alarm bells the whole time.

I think that knowing, that gut instinct, is why I kept at swimming for the 13 years it took me to win a gold medal, from 2008 to 2021. There were so many lows, and the only reason I didn't quit is because inside, deep down, I had a *knowing* that I could win a gold medal. I just needed to figure out how to do it. It drove me so much because I felt like it was bigger than me. I didn't have a choice, I just had to keep going.

I was so unconfident as a teenager in using my voice, and I would get quite frustrated with myself because I always had a feeling deep down as to what I was capable of.

I always had a confidence deep inside me, I just didn't know how to get it out.

Now, when there is a signal from my gut, or a niggling voice in my head, I listen. I notice the tiny signs that come my way, where previously I ignored them. It has given me so much comfort, taken away a lot of stress and anxiety wondering over what-ifs and why-is-this-happenings. When challenging things happen, now it is easier to trust that better or bigger is coming, or that it's because I'm on the wrong path and I need to go this way instead of that way.

The more you can develop this sense of trust, the more it becomes like a compass, making you more grounded, revealing to you when you are going in the right, or wrong, direction.

For me, the universe, or what I believe in, whatever we want to call it, is an energy. Trust in yourself and the people around you, those who are on your vibe, who have the same kind of energy as you. Who lift you up, rather than bring you down. When it comes to friendships and people you spend time with, it's about finding people in your life who make you feel good and who don't drain your energy. Obviously there are certain situations that *will* drain your energy which you have no choice over, but it's about protecting your energy as much as possible, and only giving it to things that fit your purpose.

Listen out for guidance. For the signs that will reveal there's a path, or an end goal laid out for you. Tell yourself, *the universe brought that to me for a reason, because I need to learn something here.* I call it the universe. I guess it's probably what other people call God.

Having a clear goal in mind helps with the process of knowing what a good sign is, or identifying when something is guidance. When you have written down your goal, and really commit to it, you're going to automatically choose the route that will best lead you to that objective. And I think that's nearly what gut instinct, and the signs that you're looking out for, can be at times. I think there could be a million and one things happening in front of you, but you're looking out for something specific, so you're not going to see all the other things that are happening. You're only going to be looking for that one little thing that aligns with the path you are already on. If you're looking for that one little thing, you're going to home in on it, because you are clear on where it is you want to go. What you are looking for, you will find.

The more I began to trust that things were happening for a reason and that the universe had a plan, the more things started to come together. I don't know if it just felt like I was taking the pressure off myself or if there is something greater out there. But it just gave me so much comfort to really lean into believing that things were happening for a reason.

If you are following this line of thinking, relying on an inner trust, it gives you that confidence to believe in it yourself when somebody questions your beliefs or questions whatever is going on. The feeling you get from that is so comforting, like being soothed from the inside out; there's a little bubble of peace within you.

Even when bad things do happen, I try really, really hard to look for the silver lining, or to look for why it's happening, what door is actually opening instead of the door that's been closed.

CHAPTER CHALLENGES

Small – Think back over your life, looking for occasions when it felt as if things were not working out, but in hindsight you can see that that was for the best. Make a note of them in your notebook. See what patterns come together, where things you thought might be right for you weren't. What do the things that were right have in common? What are they all aiming for, or what common values do they reflect?

Medium – Consider if there are any areas of struggle in your life, where something feels sticky, or consistently difficult. Be brave, and as honest as you can be. This could be really big stuff, like a relationship that feels like the foundation of your life. Consider what it would feel like to, instead of putting so much effort into trying to make it work, simply just let go? Instead of struggling to make something work, stop that massive effort. What happens? How does that feel? Where does all the energy you have been expending on this go? Can you point it inwards, or towards something more beneficial to yourself?

Big – Go for a walk or a run, or even lie on your bed, without any distractions, no music, no podcasts, and see what comes up in your mind. Think of areas around which you might feel discomfort, and don't try to solve the problem, but just see how you feel about it, beyond the noise of what everyone else says.

Dear 25-year-old me,

The world has come to a standstill. It's pretty scary. But it's teaching you a valuable lesson. You've been on the hamster wheel of sport since you were 10. When was the last time you forced yourself to take a break? You never have. You've always kept going. No matter what. Even on your 'time off', you've always had somewhere to be, something to do. And now you don't have that luxury. The world has stopped, and you've been forced to stop too. It's awful at first. You feel so lost, so confused, so without a purpose. But this is what you're meant to do. Rest.

Resting will heal you. Resting will clear the brain fog. Resting will show you what is important to you and what is not. You'll come out of this lockdown with a greater drive. You'll be mentally stronger than you have ever been before. The time away from the grind will make you realise how much you want this and how capable you are. You'll recognise what an absolute privilege it is to be a sportsperson and to represent your country. This resting period will be the making of you.

You'll begin to feel like you're living a dream. And you are. This is your dream, and you're turning it into your reality. It's you who dreamt of winning a gold medal. You dreamt of being seen as an equal in the

*world of sport. You dreamt of putting your dancing
shoes back on and learning how to properly salsa. It's
you, and it's always been you. You're the one who holds
all the magic to your happiness, and you're learning
to lean in and trust in the universe. Don't take that for
granted.*

*Thank you for being brave enough to face
the fear. Thank you for looking for the silver linings
and consistently trying to smile. You've realised the
importance of reaching out, and I'm incredibly proud of
you. You're not alone, and you never have been. You're
learning about everything that's in your control and
learning to let go of what's not. The little things make a
big difference, and you realise that.*

*I love you so incredibly much, and I'm so grateful for
the person that you are today. I think of you whenever
I'm struggling because you're my strength. You are
my reminder that I can get through the tough times.
Because of you, I believe I will be OK; I'm in control of
the direction my life takes me.*

*I love you. Thank you.
28-year-old you x*

eleven

Fuel

People who love to
eat are always the
best people.
Julia Child

At home when I was growing up, my dad always baked. I love to bake, and I learned how to initially from him. We would make apple crumble together, scones, cakes. From a young age, baking provided a means of switching off, of escapism; if I was going through exams, or something else stressful was happening in school, I would always turn to it. So food has always represented something of a comfort to me. Later in school, home economics was always one of my favourite subjects.

Because I found it so difficult to meet new people and to talk in social circumstances when I was a teenager, for friends' birthdays and other occasions I would often make the cake. It was my contribution; it meant I could give something, and then feel less pressure to have to talk too much. It was a way of making my presence known without having to be the loudest one in the room, or bear responsibility for creating all the conversation. Baking is something I have always found reassurance in, because I love being able to create food and give it to someone; people get so excited about cakes being made for them. It's a small act of love, really, or connection, and one that helped me express myself when I didn't feel able to speak up.

Maybe because of this, or because I travelled a lot from a very young age, and was therefore exposed to lots of different kinds of foods, I've never had a bad relationship with food. When I was travelling I didn't really have the luxury of being picky; that would have meant I just wouldn't have been able to eat. I had to take whatever was there, so I was eating sushi and all different types of fish from the age of 12.

I've been fortunate enough to know what good food tastes like, and to know what good food feels like; I've been so lucky and privileged to experience that. And because of that, I know what makes my body feel good. A food could be the healthiest thing in the world, but if I don't like eating it I'm not going to eat it. And vice versa, I know I'm going to feel shit if I eat McDonalds every day. And my skin's going to break out. Even if you were to look at what I'm doing at the moment on my break between event and training, I'm not necessarily eating very well, but I'm enjoying what I'm doing, and it's making me feel comforted. So I'm just going to do it.

I think the fact that I studied food helps. And maybe even being disabled and having to adapt the way I do certain things; I know that one size doesn't fit all, and I know that you can get health benefits from loads of different foods, instead of eating one specific thing that you don't like. You're able to get the nutrients from different things. So I think my understanding of food, and my understanding of how nutrition works, is why I'm very relaxed about what I eat.

I know I'm fortunate to be able to say this – I know a lot of people with body image issues can struggle with this area – but my feeling towards food is that it has given me the ability to do what I do, and the ability to love my body as well. I see it as fuel, as well as a source of comfort and enjoyment. Putting food into my body allows me to do what I need to do.

Listen to your body

I get asked regularly, 'Do you follow a really strict diet?' I think people have expectations around what a high-performance athlete's food intake is like. In fact, I'm actually training so much that my biggest issue isn't what I'm eating, but whether I'm eating enough. I like to eat relatively healthily, but it's not that I'm forcing myself to do so. It's more that I'm listening to how food makes my body feel, and responding to that. I would generally eat quite well because then I don't feel sluggish. It's about how certain foods fuel my body. That said, at other times, I might need food in a different way. There are certain foods that won't make me feel good physically, but emotionally I just might need that specific thing at that moment.

When I was doing my Leaving Cert, I was extremely stressed out. I remember telling my nutritionist at the time that I just couldn't stop eating chocolate. And she told me, 'Well, eat chocolate then. Eat as many Mars Bars as you want in a day, and we'll deal with it afterwards. You just need to get through this time in your life. Don't punish yourself for being stressed out and needing comfort.' So my focus on food isn't always about health or fitness aspects. Sometimes it's about the comfort that food can bring you at stressful times.

I think having that attitude towards food has given me more of an awareness about how food makes me feel, and what I need from it at different times. You really learn this as an athlete, what food can do. I find it incredible for example that there are certain foods you can eat to help you sleep – kiwis and walnuts, for example – because they have lots of melatonin in them. It's a lovely, practical way to look at food. It's there to be enjoyed, but also as a support, to help you feel good.

Fuel yourself

The word *fuel* seems important to me, rather than just talking about food, or nutrition. I feel like those words can feel very clinical, or even oppressive, and then people feel the weight of that, and get hung up on diets, clean eating, and other restrictive approaches to what they eat.

Fuel is something you put in your body to help it grow. I think it helps to look at it in that sort of practical way. Sometimes that might be eating healthy foods whose nutritional value helps you to do what you want to do. At other times, it might be other kinds of food that provide comfort in emotionally difficult times.

I also consider sleep to be a type of fuel for my body, something I need to put into it in order to achieve my goals, feel good, and progress in the ways I want to. Food and sleep for me have always been the reason I am able to do things; the most basic of building blocks. If I'm snappy or moody or emotional, chances are I either just haven't eaten enough, or I need to have a nap! Food and sleep are the foundation upon which everything else rests; make them your priority.

My mood is completely dependent on what food I eat. This means I like to experiment, trying out different foods and seeing which ones make me feel a certain way, picking an ingredient and trying it out in different ways.

Pressure cooker

After school, of course, I did a culinary degree. As I said in the previous chapter, I had wanted to do the communications course in DCU, but I didn't get the English grade required, so I couldn't qualify for the course. It was recommended to me that I do something I enjoyed. I had always loved food and so I thought it would be fun to study it.

The culinary course came with no pressure. That was important at that time, to have an outlet other than swimming, something which didn't feel burdensome, which came with no responsibilities or particular need to achieve. It also meant that if things didn't work out in the pool, at least my whole identity wasn't tied up in that; I had other things that mattered somewhat, beyond swimming.

That was always suggested to me: 'Make sure you have something else.' This didn't mean I wasn't committing fully to swimming, but it was important to have a life beyond the pool, to make sure that I had things other than that, because I would need to be able to walk away from it, eventually. I wasn't going to lose myself in it. I needed to keep other little fires alive; otherwise the end of my swimming career, when it came, would simply be too overwhelming.

Even before retirement it was important to have distractions. If there was nothing but swimming, I would be constantly thinking about it, and never resting, never switching off. It mattered so much, I needed other things to balance that slightly.

Before college, I had sometimes imagined I might go into baking as a career after I retired from swimming. One week into my new course I knew this would not work! Being an athlete is a 24/7 job. Being a chef is the same. It controls your life. I knew I wouldn't want to go from the intensity of one to the other when my swimming career ended. I realised that what I get from being in the kitchen, working with food, is more personal than professional.

It takes me into the moment. When I am baking or cooking at home, I need to be on my own. It's down time, I switch off, am in flow. In college, I was in a busy kitchen with 20 other people. I found it so overwhelming. I couldn't focus or concentrate; I was always so aware of everyone else around me and aware of the chef.

That's not to say I didn't take a lot from the course. You know that phrase, 'A change is as good as a rest'? College changed my environment and gave me the chance to make friends with whom I had something in common that wasn't sport. We had a similar interest, something I had struggled with when making friends in school, where you are all just there as a matter of course. I learned how to cook properly, without a recipe. I have the confidence to put together meals, often simple things with just three or so ingredients, for myself, a form of looking after myself.

Even though I don't have a business mind, because of what I learned on my course, I would have confidence, if I were to go into business now, that I have the necessary skills.

Food is self-care

I don't necessarily eat the *right* things all the time, and I don't necessarily follow what is considered best practice.

My feeling is that I'm minding myself when I'm doing what makes me happy.

If eating a certain type of food, or restricting myself from eating others, is going to make me miserable, that's not self-care, that's not self-love. In the name of balance, on the other side of the coin, if I eat all the crappy food it's going to make me feel awful, physically my energy is not going to be good, so that's not self-care either.

So when I'm making decisions on how to fuel myself, I'm listening to what I need rather than what specifically is textbook black and white. The only time I ever really follow textbook rules is when it comes to race day, or the lead-up to race day. Because I'm just so focused on what I'm doing, and my outcome, it works for me then. I can stick to things like the truly disgusting beetroot shots I need to take before I race! They're awful. But they're not a permanent thing I have to do every day – if they were, I wouldn't do it. It doesn't make me happy, and so that's not long-term self-care. But if it is just for a very brief period of time, in the pursuit of a goal, that's OK.

CHAPTER CHALLENGES

Small – Cook yourself (and, if you want, someone you love) a nice meal. It can be as simple as pasta and pesto; it is the act itself that matters.

Medium – What activity allows you to be in a flow state, fully engaged in what you are doing, present in the moment? Something that encourages you to switch off from thinking about what is coming next, and simply enjoy what you are doing.

Big – Figure out how many hours of sleep you need a night and aim to get that every night for as long as possible, then monitor how you feel.

twelve

Failure

Fulfilling your dreams
will take facing
your biggest fears,
quieting your pride,
and multiple failed
attempts. Getting
back up and trying
again is how you
become the version
of yourself who
accomplishes great
things.

Jennifer Diaz

I love failure! Well, obviously I don't love it in the moment, as it's happening. But I have learned to really, *really* love it. Because one of my values is self-growth, and failure is so important for that. Growth doesn't happen without failure. Because when you fail, and you properly examine it afterwards, failure is basically a checklist of the areas you need to improve. And that's why I nearly love failing more than I love winning. Because it's exciting.

OK, there it is in black and white, this is what needs to improve. This is what I need to do better. This is how I'm going to get there. When you examine why you failed, it can become almost like a series of signposts to send you in the right direction. I love it so much. Although, admittedly, I've taken a while to get to this point.

Learning to love it

From a young age, it was clear that when it came to swimming, I was talented. And my early wins were easy; I had this natural ability. It meant that I just assumed that it would always be that way.

I think that's why it's *soooo* important for kids to fail. If they don't, they can develop a false sense of their own abilities, of what real effort is.

Failing builds them up.

It's kind of the same with disabilities. If you bubble-wrap someone, or help them too much from a young age, you're preventing that person from trying to figure how to get things done for themselves. They need to try, fail and try again. If they don't get that opportunity to try, what happens when their carer, or the person who's minding them, and who might be the one giving them a false sense of security, is no longer there?

Only by failing will we realise how to do things by ourselves, and in doing so become stronger.

I guess as a kid I had that false sense of security, because I went to Beijing so young, had the success of that, and then just assumed it would always be that way. I hadn't yet had to work hard to get where I wanted to be, had not experienced and overcome setbacks, and so had no real idea how to improve.

But failure for me started as soon as I finished my first Paralympics, because I just didn't get any better for a *long* time.

And the harsh reality of not improving, not getting any better or faster, and not knowing how to, was that I was just so frustrated and angry at failure, because it seemed like one minute I was everyone's favourite person, and I had all this potential, and the next minute I wasn't succeeding in fulfilling my potential, I was failing to improve, failing to meet expectations. Failure was a series of frustrating dead ends.

This struggle, the repeated failures throughout my teens, was one of the hardest things to deal with. I loved swimming, the pool was a safe place for me, a haven and a home, and swimming was something I was naturally good at. I felt strong there, in a way I didn't in so many other areas of my life. But now it looked like that would be taken away from me. I was a kid, and I didn't yet understand how to learn from failure.

When I was 10, all people talked about was my potential, my potential, my potential. And I was just going upwards and upwards and upwards, making my way to the top. And then all of a sudden, I plateaued. I wasn't getting any better, I wasn't getting any faster. I just felt like such a failure.

Fail upwards

I guess that's one of the reasons I went to boarding school as well, because I felt, *maybe this is the solution, maybe this will make me better.* I did learn so much there, in terms of what it actually was going to take. Afterwards, I knew I hadn't achieved it all, and I hadn't implemented everything I had learned there, but I had learned what I needed to do.

What helped was surrounding myself with the people who were going to help me, rather than people who were just going to put the blame on me. People who took me as I was, rather than for what they thought I should be. I started working with people who could see my potential, but also who accepted where I was, rather than blaming me for where I was not.

If you are struggling with a sense of failure, feel it. Lean into that, don't forget it. I remember in 2019, I was probably at my fittest, fastest, strongest ever, the best version of myself physically that I had ever been, up until that point.

But I had an awful race, because of my emotions and my head. I got a bronze medal, I just completely bombed it, and I was SO upset. I couldn't stop crying. But my coach said to me, 'Just feel that. I want you to feel that, and I want you not to forget how that feels.' One of the photographers had captured a moment straight after the race where I look absolutely miserable, and I made that my screensaver on my phone, kept it there all the way up to Tokyo, to spur me on. Because failure is just so important, and I wanted to remember that I had failed, and what it had felt like to fail. I wanted to remember it on the days when I didn't want to go training, or I didn't want to get up in the morning. I would look at my phone and I would see that picture, and think, *I don't ever want to feel like that again.* That was my motivation to keep going.

I think if you hit failure, you need to feel it, but you also just need to see it as an opportunity to get better. If I hadn't failed, maybe I wouldn't have gone on to win the gold medal.

Failing is such a learning opportunity. It's actually exciting, because it means you're on the right path; you just need to adjust a few things. If you fail, and you don't feel anything, maybe you're not doing what you need to be doing. Maybe you're not doing what makes you passionate, and what you love. Failure can be a sign of so many things. Learn from it, rather than feeling any kind of shame.

CHAPTER CHALLENGES

Small – Think back on some times you think you may have failed, and write about them in your notebook. Sit with any uncomfortable feelings that arise. Next consider what the failure might have been telling you; rather than focusing on the negative, try to look beyond for the positive. What is the failure pointing to that you could improve?

Medium – Consider who are the people with whom you feel less than, and who are the ones around whom you feel good enough just as you are. Relationships with people who make you feel like you are not living up to expectations, and are therefore a failure in some way, might be worth reconsidering.

Big – Come up with something you feel you failed at, and give it another go. It could be a physical activity, it could be reaching out to a new friend, it could be a work situation. Allow yourself to become more comfortable with the feeling of not initially succeeding, and don't let it stop you.

thirteen

Moving

Movement is a medicine for creating change in a person's physical, emotional, and mental states.

Carol Welch

I feel it's often assumed that people with disabilities can't do things. It's the assumption we're confronted with from the beginning, an attitude of people wanting to put us in bubble wrap, being made to feel there are so many things we can't do, like movement and sport.

But I did those things, not just sport, but dancing, speech and drama. I got my confidence from moving. Because it didn't matter that I was a child or a woman with a disability. I was moving, and it made me realise all that I could do. I was trying as hard as everyone else; nothing else mattered. And I learned to love what my body could do. To become impressed by what I was actually capable of. Movement provided me with the opposite of the restrictions society placed on me, which seemed to be all about what it thought, or assumed, I couldn't do. Movement pushed the horizons of what my world could be.

Change the narrative

Besides what it does specifically for me, sport has helped change other people's narrative around disability. An example of that was when I was in my training camp in Fuerteventura recently. I was in the gym with a bunch of random people, just doing my session, pull-ups and whatever. After the end, I had just finished some pull-ups, and this guy came over to me and he said, 'You are *awesome.*' I think I changed that man's perception of disabled people by just doing what I needed to do! People can understand the effort and the skill and the power that goes into gym workouts.

If you're struggling with motivation, or building a habit, starting with research can be a good entry point. Literally *figure out what inspires you.* It could be realising you have an interest in something, and going down a rabbit hole about that. Be curious, figure out what it is that you're passionate about, have a curious mind. Take to YouTube. Search out TED Talks, podcasts. Listen to other people talk about what they're passionate about. Seeing what you respond to, what you find interesting, will help you figure out what you might become passionate about too. And if you find it really interesting, it might be because you have that passion as well. I think the first step is always to be curious, and to be open to figuring out what it is that lights you up inside.

People often ask me what sport I am going to do when I retire. I'm so excited at the thought of it. I want to go back dancing; that's where I'll get my fitness. There's a sport for everyone. You just mightn't have found it yet. So that's why it's so important to keep trying.

Occasionally people will comment on my body in an envious way, telling me how skinny I may look. I nearly get offended, but it also kind of upsets me. I'm strong not skinny, strong is the goal. I don't want people to be envious of me for being 'skinny'. When someone calls me skinny, it suggests I'm restricting what I eat. I feel like we as a society should be past that word.

I want them to recognise the strength in my body. It should be more about what my body did, not what it looks like. I actually don't care what it looks like. That's the confidence that you get from moving and from achieving goals in movement. You don't care anymore how you look; it becomes about what you can achieve. Walking up the stairs without getting out of breath or running a distance far longer than you ever imagined you could.

You get a mental confidence, but also, when you go to bed at night, you're tired. Movement and exercise just do so much for you other than help you lose weight. They help regulate your sleep, your digestive system, your hormones, all those healthy things inside of you that you aren't even aware are happening when you move.

I can't sit still. I was always like that – when I was in school I really struggled to think about the CAO and what I wanted to do when I finished school. Just the thought of having to sit at a desk, nine to five, Monday to Friday, seemed impossible. It's another reason I chose a culinary course – I knew I would be moving.

I cannot wait to add more variety to my movement after I retire, just have different things to do. I've kind of struggled, as an adult, with doing the same thing a lot of the time. When I think of retirement, I want to learn how to run, I want to do all the different exercises and activities. Our bodies are made to move.

When I was a kid, I'd always be in the sea. And that isn't because I love the water. It was because I loved moving in the sea and I loved playing. Even as an adult when lockdown happened and I couldn't swim, I was on a bike.

Mix it up

On Sundays, because I don't swim, I'll bring my dogs for a walk on the beach, or I might do some yoga, or I'll figure out something else to do. I just constantly have to do something.

There's also the escape movement gives from technology.

The thing is that once you start moving your body, you forget about perfectionism, and all that's important is moving in that moment. Being in your body, moving it, takes you out of your mind but also, kind of ironically, makes you forget to worry about your body, and only focus on what it can do. Class!

I know a lot of people are afraid of the gym, because they have an insecurity around not knowing what they're doing, or doing something wrong, or being looked at. And obviously there are certain skills that you need, and certain techniques, but you will also find that you figure that out the more you're moving. When I do an exercise for the first time, I am shocking at it – so bad. But then it will quickly become my goal to figure out how to do it properly.

And there is such a level of satisfaction you get when you hit those goals. Goals don't have to be hitting a certain time, or even earning a certain amount of money, or looking a certain way. They can just be figuring out how to squat properly, or how to do a dance move properly. There is immediate positive feedback that you get from these things. Even just feeling your blood pump through your body.

I know when I retire, I'm going to get to the point where I will never be as fit again as I am now. I could be, but I probably won't maintain an athlete's fitness. It's not about that though; it's about being able to walk a flight of stairs without having to think about it, it's being able to lift things, even carrying my shopping. Just going for a walk and being able to talk during the walk, or getting in the water and not being afraid that I can't swim, or things like that.

I'm so excited about being able to choose what my movement is after I retire. I want to go back dancing, I want to do more gym, I want to cycle places. The hardest thing about what I do is that it requires so much energy and so many calories, if I were to expend my energy on something else, that would affect my training. I always have to be really mindful of where I put my energy, because I need it for swimming and training. So it will be really exciting to just exercise for fun. Or just to learn a new skill. I'm so ready for it.

It's about trusting that your body knows what to do. And using movement to try new things.

Swimming is an individual sport, and I know I'm always going to be an individual athlete, but I'm really excited about joining a team sport when I retire, because I want to have that experience of being in the group. So even though it won't be my sport, and I mightn't be very good at it, I'm looking forward to making a group of friends from it and having experiences with them.

When you have a trainer, or someone expecting you to be there, it makes it so much easier to turn up because you're accountable to them. If you've committed with someone else, it cuts back on the mental energy used to just get yourself to whatever the sport or exercise is that you want to do. And then you're in the moment and you're getting lost in it.

Whenever something bad happens in my life, swimming is my saviour. I can sometimes go on autopilot, and the only escape I have is sport. I take my emotions and put them into swimming. I find this can be a really healthy way to regulate my emotions.

The simplest solution I find when I'm kind of stuck, and all I want to do is stay inside and sit on the couch and watch TV, is to just put my runners on. Because if you have your shoes on, you're not going to be comfortable in your house. When you have your shoes on, that's the first step. You're going to be standing. Even if you're just walking around the house, it can nearly motivate you just to clean your house. It's still in some way moving. And then take the next step of just going for a walk around the block.

Whenever I have a fight or I'm sad about a situation, I don't really respond until after I have swum. It helps me clear my mind. We need time for our rational brain to come in. I think that's what movement does. It gives you the space and time, and when you're in the flow of something, your confidence and your equilibrium start to come back.

Sometimes, with my ADHD, I get that paralysed thing of not being able to get started. And the only way I can zone that out is to put headphones on. Once I have music on, and I'm dancing around the place, I feel better. I have to zone out from the rest of the world. And just be in my body.

CHAPTER CHALLENGES

Small – Dance around the house listening to music. Tidy at the same time if you feel like it, although that's not necessary! Just get your body moving, and notice how your mind feels afterwards.

Medium – Find a movement buddy. Someone to go for a walk with, a run, a game of tennis, a swim. Make a plan, commit to it, do not cancel.

Big – Join something. This might feel daunting, but research it properly, and you will find some group that suits you. Give yourself a proper chance to experience the joy of movement with others, the sense of belonging, the camaraderie that comes with being part of a team (even a non-competitive one). There is little like experiencing the highs and lows of physical activity together.

fourteen

Believe

In moments when you find yourself looking for just one person to believe in you, look in the mirror, and be that person for yourself.

Kylie Francis

When I was a kid, my family didn't have a Sky Box, but I had friends who did. Going over to their houses to see the Sky channels would be such a treat; to me, Sky was huge.

When I was 21, after the Rio Games, I was made a Sky Sports scholar. It was quite a tough process: they had an open application for the UK and Ireland and there were only about 12 finalists. It was a three-year scholarship, where we got to learn about all forms of media, how to present ourselves and how to communicate efficiently. I loved it. It was a huge opportunity for me, a real boost to my confidence to be chosen by such a huge organisation.

The man who ran the programme used to be a top coach in British Athletics. Part of his job was to spot talent. Whenever I was struggling with myself, he would say to me, 'Come on, you need to believe in yourself.'

Nowadays, I like to stand out. I love wearing colourful clothes, I like to pick outfits that will mean I stand out from the crowd, I find it fun. This *really* wasn't always the case. For a long time I struggled with self-belief, and laboured under imposter syndrome, something I still deal with on occasion. When people react in a big way to some of the things I have achieved, I often feel, *oh, well anyone can do what I do*. I don't necessarily think what I do is that special.

When I struggle to believe in myself, and to find self-belief from within, it helps sometimes to look at the people who back me: my professional sponsors, the people who believe in me.

I look at the people around me and tell myself they can clearly see something that I can't see.

Self-talk

But first and foremost, for me belief is all about self-talk. It's about recognising the power of the words you say to yourself, and making sure your inner voice is helping you believe what you are capable of. I do a lot of reflecting. I don't journal but sit with my thoughts a lot, looking at what I've done and considering how far I've come. All of this helps me to believe in myself.

Before Beijing, I had never been to a European or World Championship – that was my first big event. There wasn't anything to lose; I was a naïve kid just having fun. As such, there was never any issue with belief, it was just *go do it*.

Afterwards, between Beijing and London, I struggled. Up until then, swimming had been something I was just always able to do. But when I came home from Beijing, I had no motivation. Going from a Paralympic Games to a club gala was difficult, and I struggled to motivate myself to swim fast.

And then because I wasn't getting the results, my self-belief plummeted. At the same time, I was going through a lot of insecurity about being disabled; I didn't ever want to talk about Paralympics. Back then there was a shame associated with being a part of it, because I didn't want to acknowledge my disability.

So what should have been a huge source of self-belief was in fact something I kept hidden.

In the pool, I always had the drive to keep going; even when I was struggling with training, I felt like I belonged in the water. But deep down, my belief in what I was capable of was often challenged. I sometimes lacked very supportive coaches – on occasion, as I have said, I would just be put in the side lane and told to wear fins while everyone else was doing their main set. It felt like an approach of 'Give Ellen something to do to fill her time,' rather than coaching me specifically. It made me question myself. And it meant I wasn't getting any better. As I failed to improve on the journey to getting to London, it often just felt so pointless.

I was 17 at the London Games. I can see now that I didn't have the work behind me to pull off my goals. When I failed to make certain times that I knew deep down I should have been capable of, my self-belief continued to trickle away, almost entirely disappearing. I would then get very frustrated at my lack of belief in myself.

I hate feeling weak. And I was getting more frustrated at, as I saw it, how weak I was. After London, I decided I needed to find out how to be stronger.

My self-belief began to build significantly between Rio and Tokyo, in large part from things I was doing outside of the pool.

I'm not sure how many people watched the Rio Games in 2016. But because of the pandemic, people had nothing to do but to watch the Tokyo Games in 2021. I'm sure it was the same for the Olympics that year; people watched for the first time who probably never would have watched before. There was a lot more exposure of the Games. Before that I would sometimes wonder, *what is the point in all this? Why am I doing this?* I'd struggle with feeling validated; *it's just a bunch of disabled people swimming, no one cares.* I often didn't feel like there was a lot of support or respect for what I was doing. Then I met my agent, Sinéad, and we started working together. I started getting sponsors, getting to work with all of these brands, becoming an ambassador for different companies. The visibility and the backing made me feel like I was worth something then, and there was purpose in what I was doing.

The sports role models you looked up to when you were young, it was probably as much because you saw them in an ad, on the side of a cereal box, as from watching the sport itself. Visibility is so important.

Before Rio, I had no visibility. And then all of a sudden I was getting it, through sponsorship. The first time I felt very seen with my sponsors was with Allianz. They made an ad in which they told the story of how I was insecure as a little girl, how I hid my arm, and then how I learned to roll up my sleeve and achieve in swimming. When they came to me with a proposal, they wanted to have a little me. I was able to make sure the actress they chose had one arm as well. That was cool, to be able to give her the opportunity.

In the lead-up to the Tokyo Games, RTÉ's ad for the summer of sport included me, alongside Olympians, GAA players, and rugby stars. All of us athletes together; it was a really powerful, cool campaign.

I felt, *this is what it means to be an elite athlete*. There was a respect element that had never been there before. The outside vote of confidence really helped me to drive forward.

Obviously, though, *belief needs to come from inside of yourself.* If we really think about it, there has been a time in all of our lives where we've done something we didn't think we were capable of doing. And it's about holding on to those memories when you need them.

As a high-performance athlete, your self-belief needs to be solid. You can build it up over time; you're not going to believe in yourself by just making a decision and going with it. I think the act of talking yourself into it and talking yourself into believing in a situation is really powerful.

The more positive your self-talk is, the more positive affirmations you can say to yourself, even in your mirror and talking to yourself, the more you will believe in yourself.

Foster positivity

Before a big talk or something, if I feel those negative thoughts coming in, I'll overpower them with positive affirmations, telling myself, *no, that's silly, why would I think that of myself?* I can do this by using the right language, telling myself, *I love doing this*, or *I'm going to have a great day today*, or *today is going to be really good*, and kind of overpowering any negative.

It's important to check in to see if you have slipped into negative self talk; it's easy to be in this cycle without really noticing what has happened. I'll notice the negative self-talk if I'm genuinely looking for the bad in things. If I'm all of a sudden complaining about something all the time, moaning a lot, I'll realise I'm in a cycle of negativity, so then I'll start actively trying to stop complaining about things. Or I'll call myself out.

During my most recent season, for example, I was so moany for a couple of months. I walked in one day to my teammates in the changing room, and I said, 'I'm so sorry I've been complaining so much, I'm going to try to do better.'

One of the girls that I swim with, Amy, just puts people in such a good mood with her positive energy. It's not that she's happy all the time, but she's just so good at recognising the fact that her energy is going to affect other people. I'm going to try and be more like Amy!

When it comes to performance in sport, you control the controllables. That's what all these chapters are about; what are the things throughout my career that I have had control over? My belief in myself often comes from controlling the controllables.

You could wake up in the morning and think, *I'm so tired.* But you have had eight hours of sleep, so actually you're well rested. On those occasions, I need to talk myself up, tell myself I'm actually physically capable. It's about finding the proof of the positive over the negative, because there's always going to be evidence there.

I think the majority of the things I do are for a bigger purpose than making an income or anything; what drives me is never an extrinsic thing, or a reward. I always feel like there's a bigger purpose to what I'm trying to do. That humbles me and helps me to believe in myself. I believe I'm a good person.

I'm really excited for September, to begin training for Paris – because that's the final chapter for me. I believe I'm capable of doing something great. And whether or not that is to win another gold medal – it mightn't be – I believe I'll be in the best shape I possibly can be. And I believe that I'm going to give it my all. There isn't really a doubt there that I'll be able to do that. Do it one last time, for one more year, and then retire.

Find inspiration

Take stock. Examine what it is that lights your fire. Whenever I am struggling with my own self-belief, or I feel like I need a bit of a push or a reminder, I'll go onto YouTube and look up motivation videos, finding that source outside of myself that will motivate me. It could be scrolling on Pinterest to find quotes. It could be in a book I'm reading. It could be in the people around me or it could be someone that I look up to. It just motivates me to try.

In order to bolster your self-worth, which leads to self-belief, sometimes I think it's so important to take a step back, look at yourself and your life and think, *is this really it? Am I content with this or what do I want? What habits are serving me, and which are not? If I was in a relationship with somebody with these sorts of habits, would I be impressed by them?* The things that you're looking for in other people, you have to be good at first yourself.

Visualising has been the most important thing for me in terms of fostering self-belief. If you can see it in your mind's eye, then you're going to be able to do it. The clearer your vision, the more you will work towards it happening.

Look after yourself, even with something as small as a skincare routine. It's just about trying to do yourself justice. And having that self-respect, which equals self-belief; I think it does kind of go back to respecting yourself. The number one problem for me for years was that I didn't respect myself. That even came across in the amount of sleep I got, or the food that I ate, or the people I spent time with, or what I did in my spare time. I know now when I'm slipping on these things because I will feel so guilty if I realise I'm not respecting myself. It's because now I have self-belief, and I will look after myself.

CHAPTER CHALLENGES

Small – Write an affirmation about yourself that helps encourage self-belief.

Medium – Remember something you once did which you thought you would not be capable of. Write about it, about what it proved you could do, what was unexpected about it, what it made you realise about yourself.

Big – Factor in an evening a week just for yourself. Even an hour. Look after yourself, whether it's making yourself a nice meal, having an early night, or an especially elaborate skin routine.

fifteen

Power

Remind yourself of what you've been able to overcome. All the times you felt like you weren't going to make it through, you proved yourself wrong. You're more powerful than you think.

Anon

My arm is my superpower. As we've seen, that *really* wasn't always the case. For years I struggled with feeling different, tried to hide or deny it. This never made me happy. In fact, the place I was happiest, the pool, was a place where I never concealed my arm.

It was only when I began to step into the power of being myself, no hiding, no denying of my differences, that I accessed my real power. It's a power that is available to all of us.

When I look back on the person I used to be, versus the person I am now, I find it really hard to recognise her.

It wasn't like the change happened overnight; it was definitely a slow burn. I remember the Christmas of my first year of college, going out with my college friends, and I hadn't thought about what I was going to wear. In the sense that I hadn't planned to wear sleeves; I just put on whatever I wanted. And when I was out with them, and we were dancing, it was in that moment that I realised it wasn't bothering me anymore. And I was happy.

I was so happy. It felt powerful, because it was like this weight had been hanging over me. And I actually didn't realise how heavy it was until then, when I felt so free from it.

Realising my superpower

It was in the aftermath of my TED Talk that I realised my arm could be my superpower. I was asked to give the talk, which I called 'My Lucky Fin', after my interview with *Winning Streak*. Before that, I would still think at times, *oh, I'm just the girl with one arm*, or I would always question why I was being given opportunities, a kind of impostor syndrome – *why do they want me?*

I tried desperately to fit in, to be the same as everyone else, and I felt like I struggled with being really seen as a person, as myself, beyond specifically my disability.

I think that's the biggest thing that I struggled with, being seen as a person.

I would be invited to sports awards, to gala dinners, that sort of thing. Upon arriving, the person checking the names off the list would scroll through looking for my name – but a glance up, a look at my arm, and they'd realise who I was. And that really upset me, because I felt I was so much more than my arm. It would really get to me.

After I did my TED Talk in 2017, everything changed. My whole perspective shifted. I witnessed the emotion in how people responded to it. I saw the extent to which people could relate to the feelings I was having. They weren't necessarily relating to the exact experience I went through, because their experiences were of course different, specific and individual to them – no one's life is identical to anyone else's – but as humans they could relate to the emotions that went with it.

It was then that I realised being different is in fact a really important, incredible thing.

The thing that made me stand out, made me feel different, was not just what gave me my individuality; it was also a means of connection. Being different, standing out, and being honest about that, about who I was and how I felt, was a source of huge connection once I spoke up about it. It was empowering, to step openly into that, after years of hiding.

I decided any time I got invited to something, or any time I had an opportunity to be in the media, or put my body out there, I was going to make it really obvious, I was going to shove my arm in people's faces, because that was why I was being given these opportunities. So I was going to take advantage of it and make them see, not make them glance, but make them *really* see me. Make them see me as a person.

I wanted people to see I had control over what they saw. That rather than shirk or shun attention, allow it to creep up on me in moments of unkind or unthinking comments from others, I was going to step into it, in my own way. Getting my tattoo on my arm was part of this – I'm going to make you look at my arm. I'm not going to let you decide to stare at my arm. I'm going to *make* you stare at my arm. This is on my terms.

There was power in taking control, in owning my narrative. It felt like I was taking charge of what I wanted people to think about me, and no longer allowing them to make assumptions about me.

Comfortable in your own skin

I began to feel really happy and comfortable. For so long I had struggled with not feeling comfortable in my skin. I didn't feel at ease with who I was, I didn't *know* who I was. And it was only when I really started to embrace being different, and joking about the perks of being different, and seeing the power that comes with addressing something and taking ownership of it, that I did begin to feel a sense of comfort with myself. That was one of the biggest turning points for me, figuring out how to be comfortable and how to be myself. Without being afraid of what people might say.

Now, because I have followed this path, there's not really anything you could say that would hurt me. Because I've done so much and loved my arm so much, it just couldn't hurt me because I wouldn't be *able* to believe it.

That said, there are still moments in my life even now where I flash back to feeling like that girl again, and it can be really hard to accept that what confidence I've gained isn't one-size-fits-all, durable for every situation.

Naturally, I'm a pretty chatty, bubbly person, but there are still situations now where I'll be really quiet, because I feel like I don't belong, and I'll be uncomfortable with how quiet I am. I maybe feel like I don't relate to these people, I might begin to think less of myself. Almost like impostor syndrome.

But then I remind myself, confidence and self-esteem are probably things that we will always have to work on. I know mine are; like all of us, I am a work in progress. It wasn't as if I figured out how to accept my arm and my body, and then I became the most confident person ever, the end. That is nobody's story.

In certain situations, I'm really confident because I've worked on those settings specifically. I'm confident at public speaking, I'm confident at interviews, I'm confident at my sport, I'm confident at what I can do in the gym. I've pushed myself, worked at it, and expanded my comfort zone to include these situations.

Dancing with the Stars

But at other times, my confidence can desert me. Taking part in *Dancing with the Stars*, for example, shook me a little bit. I went into it feeling really confident and then I realised, there was nobody like me to compare myself to. This was starting from scratch. This was a new beginning, the extent of which I hadn't realised until the show had already begun.

I guess because I had been in the same environment for such a long time with sport and with swimming, I felt I had succeeded to a large extent in trying to change the narrative about people with disabilities. I felt like I had nearly conquered that in sport. I'd also conquered my own insecurities in sport, and I was just so confident. I really expected it to transfer over to this new arena.

But all of a sudden I was in a new environment, doing something new, with people who had never worked with a disabled person before. It was really daunting to me that I had to teach these professionals that it was OK to hold my arm, and it was OK to challenge me, and that I *wanted* them to challenge me, I wanted them to push me. I found that kind of upsetting. I was surprised by it, but also frustrated with myself that I was surprised. And I felt sad that what I thought was my reality, that feeling that I had conquered this kind of thing, wasn't real. The people that I worked with were so adaptable, though, and would listen to me and wouldn't be afraid. But in the very beginning, it just kind of jarred me that I felt like I had to say those things.

I probably should have thought a little bit more about it in advance, and prepared myself a bit more in terms of my self-talk and envisioning what could happen. Instead, I was thrown. There were moments where I felt that I couldn't do it, where I felt so uncomfortable and unconfident, and as if I didn't belong. I felt powerless. I didn't feel like myself; that's an awful feeling.

Feeling powerless is an awful feeling.

You feel out of control, and that's a big thing to me. I think that's where I get my confidence from, feeling I'm in control of a situation. That I'm controlling the narrative, and that I feel as if I know what I'm doing. So when I feel out of control, it's like the power has been taken from me, and the rug pulled from beneath me. When things happen, even if you look at break-ups, or something not going your way, it's deeply upsetting, and you can feel so powerless that there was nothing you could do to prevent that. But sitting with that, and acknowledging that it was out of your control, is how you learn to forgive yourself and move on from it.

But in those moments, if you can find a sort of acceptance of where you're at and promise yourself that it's OK and that you're going to work on it, that is a first step to dealing with those feelings. Know they will pass.

For me now, the most important thing is being an individual, working on my individuality, and that people see me as an individual.

That's where you become powerful.

What powerful looks like

To me, a powerful person is someone who is decisive but kind, someone who is very aware of themselves, and very self-confident – but who takes the time to give a little bit of themselves to other people. I think when you're powerful, you can be seen as being intimidating; people are really intimidated by successful people, and when you take the time to show you're human, sharing emotions and being relatable, I think that's very powerful.

I don't like being fussed over by strangers. To me, my life has been very all over the place. I just don't see anything special about what I've done, or the life I've lived. Maybe it's the people-pleasing thing in me, but I don't like people feeling 'less than' because of me. I think it's also because I've been through that, I have felt 'less than', less worthy. I've been in relationships with people who weren't kind, and I've come across so many unkind people that I like to be relatable to people. Kindness is important to me.

So I don't like people making a fuss. It's different when it's kids, because kids have their own way of imagining things, and I love meeting kids who might have been inspired by my story. But generally, it's just so important to me not to take up too much space, so that everyone has the same amount of space.

The first thing you can do is find a way of giving back. By giving back, you begin to step into your power,

because you start to realise how valuable you are as a person.

We can feel at our most untouchable when we are surrounded by the people we have made connections with, and we're giving back to people. It's a celebration of your people; I think a lot of people can get that from finding and giving back to whatever it is that they're struggling with. It's like facing the fear and seeing it's not that scary, that what you're going through is actually not a unique experience.

When I was a kid, I used to go to Cappagh Hospital to get my prosthetics and for physiotherapy. Years later, in my early twenties, I was visiting one day, and in the same section as me was a woman with her one-year-old baby who also had one arm. The woman had never seen someone before who looked like her baby.

One of the doctors asked if I would like to go in and talk to the mom. Of course I said yes. As we sat chatting, I put up my arm and her little baby also put up her arm. We touched arms and the baby started laughing and smiling. And the mom – the mom burst into tears. I think in that moment, she realised her kid was going to be OK.

That kind of moment is so powerful; it really motivates me to keep going and to keep being positive. Obviously you can't be positive all the time, but you see the benefits of knowing that you're not alone. When you lean into the differences, and own

POWER

223

the differences, it takes away any power people have over you, and instead plugs you into a kind of communal, collective power, passed back and forth between people.

If someone says, 'Oh, look at her, she has one arm,' and I'm like, 'Oh yeah, I know I have one arm. It's right there,' I've taken the power back immediately. Nothing they can say can hurt me.

Whereas if someone was like, 'Oh my God, look at her, she has one arm,' and I acted as if it was the elephant in the room, and I didn't address it, I'm allowing myself to be diminished.

In the world of sport, you are constantly comparing yourself to other people. When I feel a little bit anxious or insecure, I remind myself of how strong I am, or how powerful I am. I might just say it over and over and over again. *I'm strong, I'm powerful, I'm fast. I belong here.* I will always fall back on affirmations.

I'm one of the oldest on our team now, and one of the things I often say to my younger teammates is – embrace the puke. Embrace the puke! Chase that level of uncomfortableness where the prospect of something makes you feel as if you might be sick, because when you get there, you realise, *Oh, I'm actually able to do this.* And it's always your mind that will give up before your body does. Our bodies are so much more resilient than we give them credit for. It's our minds that play the tricks on us. So we have to play tricks on our minds.

Young people are incredible because they haven't experienced enough life yet to have doubts. When I was in Beijing, I was fine, no nerves, because I hadn't experienced anything like it before, and I hadn't had people tell me how scary it is, or tell me about pressure, or expectations, or things like that. But, when it came to London 2012 and Rio 2016? So, many people had put negative thoughts in my head and planted the seed of negativity. Even just by asking me, 'Oh, are you scared?'

Like, I *wasn't* scared, but *should* I be scared?!

People don't really mean to plant the seed of doubt; I don't think they even realise they are doing it. You have to be stronger and recognise the facts that are in front of you. Think more logically and try not to let other people's emotions and fears impact how you live your life. I think that can hold people back a lot, especially when you think about the Leaving Cert. Those students go into sixth year having every single person tell them, 'Oh, how are you feeling about the Leaving Cert? Oh, it's really hard. Oh, you're going to feel so good when it is finished.' So you're just terrified before it even begins. It's about figuring out ways of blocking out that sort of noise. You can do it by just sticking to your routine and doing all the little things right.

Getting comfortable with being uncomfortable

When those about you are reacting in fear, it's just about being as practical as possible and recognising that other people are going to have opinions and thoughts and fears, but they're not necessarily the truth.

It's about getting comfortable being uncomfortable. There is always that moment before you begin something where you're hesitant and feel, *oh, I really don't want to do this*. In that moment, it's just about beginning. When you do, initially it might feel awful – *I don't want to do this*. But then you start realising what you're actually capable of doing. Then you might begin to think, *I wonder how much further I can go*. So you push yourself that little bit more, and then you start to feel the pain, to feel even more uncomfortable in your body. And that's when you're like, *OK, but this is more than I expected I could do.*

That's how you build resilience, just challenging yourself to keep going. Feel the pain and recognise, *OK, this is doing what it's supposed to be doing, and I'm going to push myself to see how far I can go*. I'm nearly wanting to feel sick. Confidence and self-esteem are built out of pushing yourself, impressing yourself with what you can do.

CHAPTER CHALLENGES

Small – What is one thing you might have been denying about yourself? How does it feel to stop fighting against this, and instead say, even to yourself, 'Yes, this is me, this is who I am'? Even if right now you don't particularly like it, just accept that this is who you are.

Medium – Try to notice when the opinions and thoughts of others are overwhelming you and see what happens when you detach from those. Listen more passively, maybe don't feel the need to fill certain people in on everything you are doing. Instead go inwards, and tell yourself you know you can do it, that everything will work out.

Big – Set yourself a challenge this month, be it physical, social, work-related. Something that makes you feel nervous as to whether you can actually pull it off. Embrace the puke!

sixteen

Belong

True belonging
doesn't require you to
change who you are;
it requires you to be
who you are.

Brené Brown

The first time I met my coach Dave, I was eight, and on my first international trip to a junior swimming competition. Dave, who would have been 24 then, is a Paralympic gold medallist, he won gold in 2000, and I think they brought him as an experienced athlete for the rest of us to see what could be achieved – he did a bit of coaching.

Dave retired after Beijing in 2008, so his last Games were my first.

After London in 2012, I asked for his help. I knew I had this potential, but I was really struggling and I couldn't access it. I didn't know how to work hard. I would always show up, but I'd always have an excuse, or I might be sick, and I would really run into difficulties in training.

As I mentioned earlier, I also still had a sort of entitlement left over from Beijing, and being sent to a Games at such a young age. I didn't understand what hard work was, and I didn't know how it felt to push my body. I think I had a kind of fear narrative around doing hard sets as well. The set could last maybe an hour and I knew it was going to hurt. But it's training, it's to help you develop and grow, and to do that, you need to push yourself. I had a negative mindset, though – *oh, this is really hard* – that turned into thinking, *I don't think I can do this*. Or I'd try and find an easy way out.

I knew something had to change, because I wasn't getting any better.

I didn't think Dave would take me on, but I asked for the meeting, and told him, 'Look, I know I can do better. I just don't know *how* to do better.' And Dave said, 'Come and swim with me.' He also said that he was taking a risk and that he didn't know whether it would pay off. A gamble – he was taking a gamble with me!

Although, unlike other coaches, he would never shout at me, we would have clashed a bit at times before I moved to his club, because I didn't know how to work hard. I was this athlete who had loads of potential but wasn't fulfilling it.

But when I moved to the NAC swim club, I was given a new beginning where I could start fresh and really work towards becoming a better athlete. I had a coach who took me seriously and trained me properly.

Since Beijing, a lot of people knew who I was. I was kind of good to have on your team, in a way – Ireland's youngest ever Paralympian. And if people didn't invest in actually teaching me, it was a kind of, 'Oh, Ellen is going to go to the Games either way, it looks good for me' sort of thing. I felt like that was the attitude with a lot of coaches I had.

I would put their club on the map, rather than them investing in me.

Finally fulfilling my potential

Dave took me seriously. He saw me fully, not just as some sort of mascot or token, but as an athlete who had serious potential. He also knew that we needed to go back to the absolute start, and made it feel safe for me to do that.

I really didn't know how to work hard until I moved to his club. But I really enjoyed it. It also kind of took the pressure off because I felt like I was a beginner again, which meant I could make mistakes. It was OK to make mistakes and to not know. I had started off as a kid in an adult world, being treated as an adult and expected to just know things. I had kind of been on a hamster wheel of Games, Games, Games – and it was like everyone expected me to just know things. I was put into an adult situation and expected to know all the answers. And I would think to myself, *but I don't know.* When I started working with Dave, he knew I didn't know. We stripped everything back.

He told me, 'We need to go back to the basics and teach you how to swim properly,' because no one had really taught me. I guess when they watched me swim, it was just like, 'OK, she can do what looks the same as everyone else.' But Dave knew how I needed to do things differently.

In Paralympics, athletes who are born with a limb missing tend to be slower than athletes who were born able-bodied and had an accident where they lost a limb. In the latter group, their minds, their brains, understand what it is to have all of their limbs. Their muscle memory still remembers how to be efficient in the water with all your limbs. Whereas for me, I've never had that. So, actually, my left arm will never understand the right way to move in the water. I really have to train that, because it doesn't come naturally to me.

Dave understood that. His attitude was, 'That's OK, we can just start from the beginning, it's OK.' I started to really enjoy training, because I understood how to push myself and I could see my times improving. Momentum started to build, and I began to want to be better the next week and the week after.

As the weeks and months passed, I really started to feel like I belonged. I wasn't the only Paralympian at the club; over time there came to be three or four of us. But all of his swimmers in the club who are able-bodied kids understood what Paralympics was because of Dave, and they understood why there were disabled athletes in the club and the competitions that we were training for. I never felt like I was in the way, because they automatically would just overtake me in a lane. Whereas in my old clubs, if I knew someone was behind me and they were faster than me, I would stop at the wall and wait or I would get out of their way.

In Dave's club, I never had to get out of anyone's way. It was like driving: they would just overtake. That's what his swimmers did. It was an automatic thing, and it was a respect thing. It was like, 'They're working and doing their own thing, and I'm doing my own thing. In this environment that we are in, we always respect each other.'

As well as Dave, I also train with Hayley Burke. She's so good technically, and so skilled: she really watches the strokes, knows how to change them, to make them more efficient. She has taken a real interest in developing coaches for future athletes. She has trained coaches all over Ireland to understand para swimming and para sport, and how to train a para body. So the issues that I had when I was younger, in terms of being put in the side lane, and not having any specific training or coaches who understood how to train me, that's a problem that Hayley is solving now, which is amazing.

I also had to learn how to train; I had never really done proper gym before. This was when I started using the Sport Ireland Institute gym.

A sense of belonging

Dave also coached modern pentathlete athletes. In modern pentathlon, swimming is one of the five sports. Five of them trained with us twice a week. Of the five, two of them went to the Olympics, so it was around this time that I started training with Olympians as well. In the beginning, it was just in the pool, but then I started using the Sport Ireland Institute gym, which is where every athlete from all different sports trains.

They would run cooking demos, educational workshops, lots of events, so you'd spend a lot of time meeting different athletes and getting to know them. The conversation would often focus around each person's main event, and you would follow each other's progress. There was so much similarity between our calendars, even though we were different. And we would watch each other's progress in the gym. I learned how to do cleans, a movement involving flipping a weighted bar, using my strap. I would be beside Olympians or other athletes who couldn't do that, so respect would form.

Any Irish sportsperson that I've spent time with has seen me as an equal and made me feel like I belong. I train in the Sport Ireland Institute campus; Olympians and Paralympians train side by side. All you are is an athlete. You're going to different competitions, but you're seen as elite athletes and there are standards that people expect of you. So an Olympic athlete sees me as an equal; they are my allies because they understand.

Irish Olympic athletes and Irish sportspeople really understand Paralympics and really respect it. When they see an athlete working hard, they understand that. They know that my fellow Paralympians and I belong within their ranks.

Especially for Rio in 2016, there was a group of us training throughout the summer, Olympians and Paralympians, all hoping to get to the Games. After I won my medals in Rio and then in Tokyo, Natalya, one of the pentathletes and Olympians in that group, was covering the Paralympics for RTÉ. She was the first person I spoke to for an interview after my race. She understood the work that had gone into this achievement, so that was really special.

Tokyo was the first Games where I saw the Olympic rings and the Paralympic logo side by side. At the Olympic Games, the rings are everywhere. There are specific traffic lanes for the Olympic buses because they need to get to venues on time. There are signs and merchandise everywhere. During the break between the Olympics and Paralympics they change all the logos, the road markings, the signs; they have to change everything to the Paralympic logo.

But then in Tokyo, the logos were side by side for both Games. It wasn't just during the Paralympics, but during the Olympics, too. It made me feel very proud and respected, like we were finally being seen as equals.

In Ireland, it felt like there was an element of people not understanding the Paralympics because of the lack of media coverage and exposure of para sport throughout the four-year cycle. People didn't get to see Paralympians work hard. All they saw was every four years, this competition after the Olympics where disabled people were competing. It's very hard to see that as high performance, because there was nothing for them to compare it to. They didn't understand what a fast time could be.

The gym itself is probably the best way of showing the ability of para athletes, because most people can't do a pull-up, and I have one arm and I'm doing weighted pull-ups. It's one of the reasons why I post some of my gym workouts on my Instagram. That exposure helps people understand what is involved. People understand heavy weights. Even if you don't go to the gym, you still understand what 100 kilos is, and you still understand the size of weights.

They understand the training and the adaptations because they see it. How does she do a pull-up with one hand? Because I have a strap, or my gym prosthetic. Seeing the adaptations that I'm making helps people understand that this is high performance.

Finding my voice

When I started to find my voice and started talking about my arm and about the Paralympics, and I started getting sponsors, I began really loving what Paralympics was. Because the Paralympics is about showcasing what people with disabilities can do, and it tries to help society to understand what is possible.

Sometimes it's nice that people can't see the difference between an Olympian and a Paralympian, but calling me an Olympian is also taking away my identity as a disabled person, because I'm never going to make the Olympics. I'm never going to hit those times. And the training I do, I have to adapt every single day, and I have to do things differently. In the Olympics, it's kind of like, 'Who can do this the fastest?', whereas in the Paralympics it's, 'Who can find the fastest way to swim this?' That's why identifying as a Paralympian is so important to me, because it's an obstacle course to get to the finish line.

Whereas the Olympics – obviously I know everybody is different and people have different strengths and weaknesses, but at the end of the day they're kind of still all working towards a very similar way of doing things, to get a similar result. Whereas in Tokyo, for example, I have one arm, I raced for gold against a girl with one leg, and both of us were swimming differently and had to adapt differently in training, to figure out how to get the gold medal or get a similar time.

I remember kids in school asking, 'How do people in wheelchairs swim?' They get out of their wheelchairs! The kids were so surprised. I remember thinking, 'Their wheelchair's not attached to them, people can get out of their wheelchairs.' It's a thing where people can't see beyond the disability. As soon as people are aware of a disability, that's all you are, and I knew that, so I didn't want to be reduced to just that one thing about myself. That's why I felt so strongly that I didn't want anyone to know I had a disability. I didn't want to be the girl with one arm, I just wanted to be Ellen.

Even now, I'm 28, and I've had people, really, really lovely, well-meaning people, come up to me and say, 'I don't even think of you as disabled.' As if they are saying something positive. I find that so offensive because it's who I am. I always say that I've not had to overcome my disability, I've had to overcome ableism, and when you say you don't think of me as disabled or I'm not really that disabled, you're taking my identity away from me and you're belittling the experiences I've had – but you're also making it a bad thing to be disabled.

I want to stand up and proudly say I'm disabled, and for anyone seeing the things that I'm doing as a disabled woman, I hope that it will give them a bit more pride around acknowledging their disability. Because I had none of that. There was no pride about being disabled.

I've been told by professionals that I'm not disabled enough, or by staff at concerts that I'm not disabled enough for a certain entrance. My identity has been questioned so many times. I remember when I was about 12, and we were on a training camp, we had a day off and we went to a water park. The rule was that disabled people got free entry, so all the para athletes were going in and I was one of the last to go in. They were like, 'Oh no, you need to pay, you're not disabled enough.'

I started driving when I was 17 and I had to get adaptations to my car. In order to pay for them there's this grant you can get from the government, but in order to get that grant you need a blue badge. So I applied for it.

I was denied it, and so went for a review in front of three doctors, who essentially decide whether or not you are disabled enough. One of the doctors, a man in his fifties, started asking did I wear a prosthetic? I told him I didn't, that I don't like prosthetics, I'm not very good at using them and I don't like how they look or how they feel, and it's not who I am.

He started lecturing me about why I should get one. That you can get really lifelike ones now, and if I got one, no one would ever know I had one hand. I was 17 when he said that to me. And that just sent me down the rabbit hole again. There have been so many times where either I'm disabled, or I'm not disabled enough. And both were bad. That's why it's so important for me now to claim it.

I'll always be someone with a disability. I'm hoping things will be different for the generation that comes after me, but I'm always going to be Ellen, the girl with one arm, because as much as we are learning to accept things, society is still not there yet. So I still have that role, that responsibility, and the job of getting it there.

I've been in sport for so long now and I've seen the change with each Games and how athletes are treated after each Games.

In London 2012, there was an ad on Channel 4 which called Paralympian athletes superhumans. And as much as it kind of excited people about the Games, I didn't really like the term 'superhumans' because it was in a way romanticising the elite disabled. Kind of putting down regular disabled people; the only acceptable level of disability is a Paralympian, because they're strong and they're physically able.

I think a lot of disabled people find the Paralympics very frustrating, because random people might ask, 'Are you in the Paralympics?' Even a disabled person in a gym or in a pool, a lot of people would have been approached and been asked, 'Oh, are you a Paralympian?' It takes away what it actually takes to be a Paralympian, but it also puts unnecessary pressure on people with disabilities, especially kids. If an able-bodied kid is having fun in sport, you wouldn't automatically go to them and tell them, 'You're going to the Olympics.' Because there's very few people in the world who achieve that goal. It is understood what is involved in that. Whereas people feel the right to say it to disabled kids. And then that puts unnecessary pressure on them, and they fall out of love with the sport because it becomes all about pressure and achieving.

How do you feel like you belong? I think the first thing is finding something that you love doing and immersing yourself in it. Get lost in it. People can then see how capable you are, and what you're able to do. This way you will be able to find your people and your space in the world.

Perfectly imperfect

I had used the hashtag 'perfectly imperfect' since around 2016. Because life is so messy and there's no one way of doing things. What holds us back is when we try to do things perfectly. And then we are hard on ourselves for not being perfect. Instead, try to learn to love the imperfectness of things – that's how it becomes perfect, in a way, because nothing is perfect.

You become perfect by recognising how imperfect you are.

I tried so hard as a teenager, and in sport, to be perfect. The more I forgave myself for not being flawless, or this imagined vision I had held, and the more I just kind of embraced being different, and doing things differently, and seeing the joy of being successful while being different, the more I really connected with the phrase *perfectly imperfect*.

It's really liberating when you lean into the imperfectness of things. I am much more comfortable wearing no makeup, posting a picture of myself as I am right now, hair damp and scraped back in a bun, face clean but free of anything, than some perfectly captured 100-takes-to-get selfie. Because I think once you set the impossibly high standard of perfect, you're always chasing it. And you're always trying to be perfect, but never succeeding. It is setting yourself up for failure. When I was a teenager, I used to straighten my hair for two hours and then take an hour to do my makeup. And it would be because I was trying to be flawless. Whereas now when I get dressed up, I just really enjoy the process of doing my hair and my makeup and having fun with it. But I could also easily throw on mascara and that would be it, and I would be happy and content with that.

Because I've learned to lean into the imperfectness of things. I know I don't have to look a certain way to be happy. And I don't have to do things a certain way to be happy. And even having the perfect house and the perfect clean and organised car. My car is a tip 99 per cent of the time because I live in it, and I'll most likely have four different bags of stuff in there at all times. A laundry pile will start to build up, and then someone will ask, 'Can I have a lift?' And I'm like, *oh God*. But it's just like being able to laugh at how imperfect things are.

If I'm tired, I will be a lot clumsier. Now, if I'm having dinner with someone, I will warn them, 'I'm having one of those days, chaos is just following me. Something could happen here.' And I'll end up spilling the soy sauce all over the floor or something. My favourite was being late for training and having to explain that my blender exploded and my smoothie went all over the kitchen. Just lean into the funniness of things. Be kind to yourself. It's so much easier.

Conclusion

I hope after reading this book that you feel a little bit braver. I want you to know that you're not always going to feel confident, and you're not always going to feel 100 per cent ready.

That's OK.

It's about showing up every day for yourself and just trying. Some days you mightn't want to try and that might mean you need to rest, and just have a day to yourself. And that's OK too. But the more you try, it's kind of like training a muscle; you're training yourself to love yourself and to be comfortable in your own body. And that doesn't happen overnight. That happens by showing up every day. There is a saying that in sport or in any task, it takes 10,000 hours to become an expert. And we've probably spent the majority of our lives putting ourselves down, so we're experts in being negative. That's a muscle we've really flexed and are really good at. So we need to work on those hours to be more positive and to get better. And it's just going to take time. But by taking the first step and being brave enough to try: that is how you get there.

I hope this book helps you to do that.

Dear 30-year-old me,

I am so excited to meet you. I'm not afraid of ageing. I'm actually quite looking forward to it. My biggest fear in life is not growing. Not experiencing all there is to experience in the world. And that's why I'm so excited to retire. I'm so excited for the next chapter. And that next chapter is you.

There are a few things I want to remind you of. Our mantra has always been, 'be the person you needed when you were younger', and as I am the younger version of us, here is who I need you to be.

I need you to be in love. With yourself, with where you live, with who you are with, and with the career path you choose. Love is the most powerful driving force in the world. Leading with your heart will make the hard days more manageable. It will give you purpose. It will always be your why. Life is too short to not be passionate about what you are doing. And you deserve a life filled with love and passion. You deserve to love yourself and love the only body that you have. You deserve to be with someone who also makes you feel that love. You deserve to live in a place that you feel is your home. And you deserve a career that makes getting up in the morning easy. You know what it feels like to work hard. You've done it your whole life. And you know how brilliant you are when you actually care about what you are doing.

Please don't forget who you were before. Please don't take for granted how important water and swimming are to your life. Sport was your safe haven when you felt like you didn't belong in the world. Don't take that for granted. You have an incredible skill built up from years of training and it would be a shame to lose your ability in the water. Just because you don't have to turn up every day doesn't mean you shouldn't turn up at least once a week. It's important for your mind, but also important to keep your body strong. We may not be an athlete anymore, but we still have a disabled body. And we need to make sure that our body is still capable of living in the world that isn't designed for us. I love being the strong disabled girl. So do not take that away from me.

Take advantage of all of the time you now have to do whatever you want. Go out for drinks with your friends. Go dancing whenever you want to go dancing. Join a club. Make some new friends. Figure out who you are without swimming and keep growing. Learn how to move your body differently, but make sure you keep moving.

I'll see you soon,
28-year-old you x

Acknowledgements

First of all, I want to thank you, the reader, for believing in me enough to buy this book. I hope it helps you in some way, shape or form in your journey to believing in yourself.

Secondly, I would like to thank Lia Hynes for welcoming me into your home and helping me throughout every step of this process. I hope I've found a lifetime friend in you, Sarah and your cats.

And to my agent, Sinéad, who will always be so much more than an agent. You are the most caring, motivational, hardworking woman I know and I'm so lucky to have you as a friend. Thank you for always looking out for me and pushing me to be my best. Your belief in me is the reason this book exists.